Reactions²

New Poetry

This exciting anthology of the UK's best new poets acts as a listening post for anyone interested in contemporary poetry. *Reactions* showcases work by up-and-coming talent; those who are at first collection stage or moving towards it. It is published by Pen&inc., a new press based in the English and American Studies department at the University of East Anglia. *Reactions* draws on talent from UEA and the rich writing community of Norwich and the region, but not exclusively: its open submissions policy has attracted writers from around the country and further afield.

Reactions is edited by Esther Morgan, a teacher of creative writing on the undergraduate programme at the University of East Anglia. Her first poetry collection, *Beyond Calling Distance*, is published by Bloodaxe (2001).

Reactions² New Poetry, edited by Esther Morgan

First published, 2001, by EAS Publishing for Pen&inc., University of East Anglia, Norwich, NR4 7TJ

A CIP record for this book is available from the British Library
ISBN: 1-902913-12-4

Production: Esther Morgan/Julia Bell
Design/Typesetting: Julian p Jackson
Copy editing: Emma Hargrave
Cover design: Julian p Jackson
Cover image: Barbara Watts

Reactions² is typeset in Hoefler Text

Printed by Biddles Ltd, Kings Lynn and Guildford

Reactions[2]

New Poetry

Edited by Esther Morgan

At the University of East Anglia

Acknowledgements

Thanks to Sally Bailey, Julia Bell, Simon Brett, Jon Cook, Magda Russell, Val Striker and Sara Wingate Gray for their enthusiasm and practical support; Julian p Jackson for his design and typesetting work; and Emma Hargrave for her copy-editing skills. Thank you to Dr Anna Garry for her helpful advice.

We gratefully acknowledge the generous financial support of the Esmée Fairbairn Charitable Trust, the Robert Gavron Foundation, and the School of English and American Studies at UEA. Thanks also to our supporters in the region: Peter Bolton at the Norfolk and Norwich Festival, Jonathan Denby at Anglia Railways and the Wells-next-the-Sea Poetry Festival.

Finally, I'd like to thank all the contributors for the pleasure their work has given me and the readers of this anthology.

Contents

Contents

Reactions²

Contents

Contents

Introduction

In his poem 'Doors', Christopher Allan suggests that poems themselves can be thresholds, ways through to different perceptions of the world. It's a metaphor I can relate to having read several hundred poems over the last few months in my role as editor of this anthology. Sometimes there has been a room on the other side, sometimes a garden or landscape; there have been doors to the past and the future, to the street outside my house, or to a strange dream world. None of the poems I have chosen are locked.

This sense of opening is an ambition of the anthology as a whole. Launched last year, *Reactions* is an annual gathering of some of the best new poetry in the country. It aims to showcase work by up-and-coming writers, those who are at first collection stage or moving towards it.

In trying to identify trends or themes there is always a danger of imposing a falsifying neatness. The diversity of *Reactions'* is one of its strengths: I simply have published poems which I regard as exciting and risk-taking. But there are some fascinating undercurrents too. Some of these come together in the last line of Julian Stannard's poem 'Ballo' which stands as an epigraph to the anthology as a whole: 'And because it is dark we are laughing.'

Poetry has always been good at tackling the dark stuff, and I was struck by the different kinds of darkness in *Reactions*: the black holes of family life, love, identity, God, death, the state of the earth and the universe. A presiding spirit for the anthology might be Stephen Hawking in James Knox Whittet's poem 'A Brief History of Devotion': the famous philosopher-scientist stares out into a darkened auditorium with eyes 'like disintegrating comets', telling jokes in his uncanny electronic voice in the face of a God who's hiding somewhere in the universe. The poem ends with the professor's desire for us 'to go on conversing/whatever the cost', and this note of defiance runs through many of the poems here.

Humour is one expression of this defiance: satirical, bitter, compassionate. There's a thrill in seeing these writers tackle the negative matter of life: from the bleak punning of Paul Batchelor's 'The Man in the Moon', an elegy for the lost underworld of the miners, to the wry wit of Dean Parkin's treatment of the ageing process in 'The Big Five-O', or Helen Oswald's robust two fingers to the insurance industry in her poem 'Assurances'. Their laughter is never merely nihilistic or defeatist, but full of energy and surprise.

Neither does *Reactions* neglect the light: the reader will find poems which celebrate moments of joy, contentment, grace. A sense of possibility finds delicate visual expression in Clare Crossman's 'The Field', or Mark Haddon's description of a winter headland in 'New Year's Day' where 'we can walk, each year,/a little further out into the fog'. This sense of exploration, of pushing the imagination further into the unknown is a quality I was looking for as an editor. Sometimes this is achieved by the writers' meticulous concentration on the world in front of them, as in Danny Hardisty's visual and psychological close-ups of family gatherings, or the intimate geographies of Andrew Waterhouse's work. Other poets draw on myth, legend and history for their inspiration, with narrators from another time and place, such as the medieval housewife in Miranda Yates's 'Savonarolla', or they invent legends of their own as in Helen Ivory's apocalyptic visions of a world which rains babies, and where a wolf eats the stars.

Whatever their tone or subject matter, the poets I've chosen open up doors and take the reader into new territories: please walk on through.

Esther Morgan, Norwich 2001

Patricia Adelman

Wanting

We sit on the love-seat
bathed in orange blossom and rose
and a blackbird's peal of welcome.
To my *Just listen to that!* you only
hesitate a Yes, Yes . . . And what I want
is to breach the world of your mind
and not to feel the rise of
aloes in my throat
at the inevitable, *Can we go now?*
Let's look at the waterfall first, I bully.
Home straight after that? you bargain.

Quick-march the short way back
by minor roads, me first across,
you dithering on the kerb
waiting for far-off traffic to pass.
Not like it used to be
when you'd be over in a trice,
laughing back at cautious old me.

The final stretch, taken at a trot,
sees you bright-eyed and breathless,
diving for the remote so as not to miss
the weather forecast,
Why? I ask.
So we'll know, you nonplus.

Three Bereavements

By shooting.
    Tim – wire-haired leaper, champion barker
trained to growl at whoever touched me – at
the hand of a farmer, *a kindness really,*
should never have been let out on the road,
who didn't shut that gate? No money for vets.
My father wept, cursed, wept afresh.

By drowning.
    Tizwoz. Me just home from school,
her yowling in the basket, ready for the canal.
Whiskers poking through the holes.
Old Blokey put her in – *such a nice old man –*
his right it seemed, she got his best layer. Regardless
it squawked and pecked free on the common.
My mother stood helpless.

By carelessness.
    Mine. Kathy's head smashed in
as she rocked off the cradle hood.
Too many pieces for the Dolls' Hospital.
I sat her on *just for a minute, only a minute,*
why can't it be only a dream? I howled into
my mother's lap. *You'll learn from this*, she said.

Needs
'A child eats breakfast in a hostel for the homeless.'

This photographer knows his Bonnard,
table filling half the space,
staging her for us – and yes, there,
cut off by the left edge, a ghostly figure
we must be meant to ignore.

Why does everything seem too big for her?
Thick cardi, sleeves rolled up to let her tackle
that dinner plate of jumbo chips.
Those sturdy fingers have to be
a trick of the lens,
though not, I think, her eyes,
diminishing her face,
looking blank side out.

She can't be more than three.
Cheeks, lips still in suckling mode.
It's a look I've seen at the breast,
bright with leftover reproach
at uncalled for delay.

I could be missing something here.
Read differently, that dewy mouth's
a defiant grin; those tragic eyes
a blank of concealed mischief;
the artful pattern of the tablecloth
a splatter of thrown food, sign of a scrap
with whoever it is that's out of sight.

But no. First thoughts stay with me,
and it's leaf dapple on that table,
filtered by sunlight through a tree
outside a wide window, where
she sits to watch the birds.

As for that Other, the photographer knows
how Mother (or whoever) has to be
ghosted out, for the sake of art,
the appeal of a lone child at table,
our need for a hint of an angel.

Christopher Allan

The Gift

It was all so long ago I've forgotten
how it started. You seemed to come
from a dream. From somewhere inside me
you eased out a hand, a shoulder, a thigh.

Trees broke through the ground, but
it was as if I'd always known leaves;
then rain gave a shine to your skin
and fruit fitted my palm with a strange exactness.

Later, when I watched you walking away
towards the light, I knew I was hollow.
I crossed the river, climbed a hill
and saw you still drifted beyond me.

Then you turned and opened your mouth
and began to sing. It was
soon after that you stole up on me,
surprising me with a gift. What could I do

but hold out my hand to take it?
There it lay, fresh and round and good.
And how sweet it tasted, though the core
was bitter and would bruise my tongue.

Since then, how many red suns have risen
over the land? How many moons
have grown and dissolved, mirroring your cycle?
Now I am old, they dissolve

into each other. Yet my love endures,
even though you now sleep under clay.
I will not let them speak ill of you.
Long ago, what you gave me was the world.

Doors
in memory of William Stafford

Silence is a door
if you sit still and wait,

and the sea, each breaking wave,
the sound of opening and closing.

There's a door in the bar of sun
that lies across the table.

There's a door in lips
when they kiss you.

There's a door hung in buttercups
and daisies if you get up close.

This candle is a door and a prayer.
My mother was a door.

A beaten drum makes a door
as the melody weaves its design.

Any dark tunnel you are in, I'm told,
has a door if you can find it.

But how can a flat with dead air
and no furniture *be* a door?

Often a poem can become a door
and sometimes, the poet.

There are doors almost everywhere,
they stand ajar and you see a light.

But when you run towards them
with your need, they always slip shut.

The keyholder cannot be found.
You wonder, *Did he enter there*

and decide never to return?
If you could somehow open one,

ease yourself through and stand up,
then where would you be?

All Poets Are Wounded Men

See that man over there
idling under an apple bough?
He is one of the wounded men.

                    You say
you see no blood
run down his sleeve, note
his face is not punctured.

But you've noticed how his eyes
light a little
like small flames fed by the wind.

Does he have a name, the wounded man?

He has told me names are not important.
He has told me merely to focus
on what is before your eyes,
                moment to moment:
cloud and star,
                hill, briar and beast;
the man feeding his computer
in the highrise made of steel and glass;
the waiting call-girl
                lovely in a red window;
or the lost child playing alone
in a puddle of petrol.

                Tell me, you say,
where is the wound of the wounded man?

For we have just seen him leave
the cool shadow of the apple tree
and venture a sunlit track
                towards the city.
He does not limp, his pace is even.
He carries nothing in his hands.

                I think his wound
festers somewhere below his heart.
The road he is on is full of ghosts
and so is the wounded man
                and so is the wind.

Liz Almond

The Cornish Pasty

I was sitting on a beach minding my own business
when the man next to me starts up this whine
from his stomach about how he's in need of a pasty
– we were on a Cornish beach –
he doesn't even notice the surf that's coming up
and when his wife arrives without pasties
things get ugly. He starts on at her
about the *terrible decisions* she's just made
concerning food, provisions. God, you'd think he was going to war
the way supplies munitioned his tongue
and you could see from the way she bent her head
she was shot to pieces, and from the way he postured
around a pile of macho stones, he the victor.
And then, when he wouldn't let things go,
the children joined in with a
Daaad, shut up, Dad, we've heard that before
and when he stuck his bayonet in some more,
the youngest, no more than three years old, chimes in with
bastard, bastard, bitch, bitch
which did silence the man for a minute as he cradled the child
and you could tell what kind of family they were
and I thought of my own talent for bitterness
and my own failed family life,
the fire and brimstone that was husband and wife;
barbed like a sea urchin in ambush for a child's instep,
broken spines eased out with oil and tweezers.

It was a bank holiday on the coast – couples and families
and I was exultant as I walked the cliffs,
swam alone, sunbathed, ignored the coastguard's rules,
flirted with rip-tides, undertows, death by drowning.

Circe's Cave
for Ruth Padel

My mother's house is a prism
hidden in a secret drawer
with spirit level and plumb line
poultry shears and garden twine.
I go to the greenhouse where Spanish tomatoes
refuse to ripen, take a fistful of basil,
breathe its purple smell.
'When a woman bends over she opens her mind,'
Ibrahim Ferrer sings, and somehow the words
offend me less in his language;
Buena Vista's music
cuts glass, turns each facet
towards my mother in her hot-air balloon
high over the house, my mother's house
which I pretend is Circe's island –
you're a good girl, my mother shouts down to me –
no I'm not, I mutter, I'm a sorceress
with her very own sea captain,
I'll keep him for ever in my cave,
feed him cheese and wild honey
until we're both becalmed.
Goody-Two-Shoes is shelling peas,
the pods will be fatter in a few days,
this is her only certainty.
The pea artillery
makes the saucepan depressed –
why not take an aspirin? it asks,
you'll find one in the knife drawer.

The Shut Drawer

My feet grope their way across warm stone,
where wild encroaches
whispering *temporary, provisional,*
we can unmake your designs.

I've been pruned, cut back, stopped.
I did, in my tracks, on the brick path
leading towards the cold-frames.
In there, ironically, heat builds
and new growth appears.
Perhaps I'll even be given a name,
a name for *untameable yet vigorous.*

Together we crunch the gravel path
to Pomona and her high priestess's hat.
To our right, beside the dredged pond,
the levitated figure is earthed
by her bronze hair rooted at both ends.
Her cherry scion is bound and bound again
by cream raffia. You run your fingers
over the Bologna cast under her Russet apple tree.
I try to pull up seedlings. Tenacity. Resilience.
Leave me alone, I'm painting, writing, mothering.

Umbilical, the pulse of blood from one
to the other. Symbiosis.
The sun goes down on our cut cord,
the cauterized nodes of separateness.
We were together by the spouting mouth,
the sound of running water
irrigates the parched selves we can become
when we desert one another.
Proximity, one more desire.

The cupboard door, the drawer,
the open drawer, her smell,
her sea-filled eyes, her face, the makeup streaks,
she's me, I'm her, we're we.
Inhaled then gone again,
the shut drawer, her red-rimmed eyes,
the loss, the dark, the sea,
shut up, the shirt, don't speak to me
like that. The sea, the tears,
the shut drawer.

Turning Turtle

A loggerhead's crazy-paving shell
tilts against the ocean bed,
her neck cranes upwards for air,
for the guidance of stars,
for the correctness of sand
scraped into a hollow
to receive her eggs.
I think of the tiny turtle nestled
in your wallet, in the small dark place
next to your groin, that's driven you
as far from home as you could get.
The *what you've left behindness* of it
wakes you in the early hours
the way a baby wakes a mother.
I've no traces, only photographs, nothing
to nuzzle into for the smell of you,
faint but always recognized.
Where is the boy with the axe?
I sit him on my knee and feed him grapes,
he tips his head to let the juice
run down his parched throat,
the boy with the axe who's not afraid to cry
has melted, slipped through my fingers

like ice or liquid wax.
Up a gum tree, I hear my father say
and see you reach into the eucalyptus
in the cool of early morning.
His words solidify in my stomach
like chewed rye bread,
dark and heavy as tar or molasses
that alters my centre of gravity.

Bucket and Spade

The daughter of a river queen
weighs out some Camembert
that runs beneath its rind.
For a moment I have her buoyancy,
whose cakes are gilded
whose fish are gutted
whose flesh is hopeful –
she's upright as a stand of new bamboo
with bands of green and purple.
She loves Rothko and Giotto,
makes haloes for herself
punched like hurdy-gurdy scores.

On the beach
a romance of bucket and spade:
Daddy digs a moat
for the sea to fill.
Father and sons gone crabbing;
soft underbelly of crab
the shell of childhood barnacled
with adult sadnesses.

On the riverbank someone else's son
is trained in the art of manliness;

I can't
You can, keep going
I'm frightened
You're not
I can't
You can you little shit,
I'll make a man of you, get on with it.

His head is under with weeds and minnows,
eyes awash with silt,
one lid hooked by careless casting
held open, shocked.

Paul Batchelor

After the Odyssey, XII
for Jeff Nosbaum

Still hopeful then of putting out, we gathered
on the quay. The south wind filled the sails, shrouds taut,
but with a stillness on the sea as though
it had been charmed. Already, fishing boats were
eagerly casing off, as if they sensed
the day would send none home with empty creel.

At length, as we prepared to put aboard,
there came one, scornful of our occupation
(old man, the skin hung loose about him)
who stood with folded arms, asking how far
we thought we'd get, so ignorant of map
& pilot book . . .?
                    'We'll have the stars to steer by.'
But what (he taxed us further) of provisions,
what bait, what nets? He kept us talking,
finding the flaws in all our arguments,
until we saw we'd missed our chance of catching
that day's omens: over the harbour, where
our single vessel bobbed, grey clouds had gathered:
sultry noon.

            I wonder: had we told
that grey old fool the purpose of our voyage;

had we but said, 'We sail in hope of hearing
the Sirens' song: Parthenope, Ligea
& Leucosia, these will welcome each of us;
their wings the silent wings of owls, their eyes
merciless as hawks . . . and don't try to
dissuade us, we who know what horrors follow
fishing boats, what swarms upon the ship-
wrecked man: the lifeless eyes, those bloodless, hanging
lips that ripple back, the grin that splits
& widens to a jagged O; we'll give
ourselves as gifts, and let this vessel be
a lure to catch our deaths . . .'
                                    We told him not.
Since then I've grown
accustomed to another song. The sea's
long burden on the land. The cry of gulls.
Remember me . . .

Transferable Skills

. . . a prickle of rain at the window. The skyline
                darkens & a last, stray
            9-5'er scurries from his office block.
A scatter of hail: a warning rattle,
                like something
        on the lung. You watch him
try to hail a taxi, squinting at
                the rain as at
        a bitter taste. Your fingers start
to tap the keys: a blur of
                tock & tick, and fifteen
        years ago, your mother
learns to type: the fumbling
                punch of keys
        yet to find a rhythm;
the tireless stopwatch

ticking underneath;
her flinch
when two keys stick. Textbook advice:
'If you complete
an exercise in time,
look back and see where you went wrong . . .'
The time she's locked
in practice; the time
she spends at her class; the time she
hammers (second
by stubborn
second) off the clock, with something like
the pleading look
of this commuter,
that makes you think
of a convict, cringing
in a searchlight's sweep.

The Man in the Moon

May every Durham colliery-owner that is in the fault
Receive nine lashes with the rod, and then be rubbed with salt.
May his arse be thick with boils so that he may never sit,
And never burst until the wheels go round at every pit.

. . . Our work is taken from us now – they care not if we die –
For they can eat the best of food, and drink the best when dry . . .

'The Durham Lock-Out', 1892

I

The man in the moon's lost his memory.
  Now he has nothing to hide.
If you wait for the clouds to melt away,

You'll see his darker side.

He'll take you in as his pupil.
  He'll teach you how to sing
The song that goes 'Poor me! Poor me!
  Poor me! Pour me a drink . . .'

He'll fix his blind eyes on you,
  Examining you as you pass:
You'll see his gaping, drowning face
  As you drain your glass.

2

The man in the moon is casting his curse:
a man shall be born with unquenchable thirst.

As babe, he'll suck & puke & cry
until his mother's tits run dry.

As boy at school, his brains will burn
& thirst for knowledge he can't learn.

As lover, wring his love's heart out
each time his own is dry with doubt.

As soldier, spit a gob of mud
& swear to drink his enemy's blood.

As miner, drink up half his pay,
then sweat it out at work next day.

So he'll drink. And drink. And drink again:
like a river drinking rain!

One day the river's banks will burst.
When that day comes he'll die of thirst.

3

While going the road to where we did part,
  Hurroo! Hurroo!
While going the road to where we did part,
  Hurroo! Hurroo!
While going the road to where we did part,
Where you spoke your mind & I sang my heart,
Whatever united us tore us apart.
O, Father, we hardly knew ye!

    When you're a spirit, when you're a ghost
    & the north wind blows right through ye,
    Remember the day you heard us say,
    O, Father, we hardly knew ye!

Why are your eyes so bloodshot red?
  Hurroo! Hurroo!
Why are your eyes so bloodshot red?
  Hurroo! Hurroo!
Why are your eyes so bloodshot red?
'When the dust gives me thirst I must drink,' you said,
(I think that's where you were misled).
O, Father, we hardly knew ye!

Why is your face so dirty & black?
  Alack! Alack!
Why is your face so dirty & black?
  Alack! Alack!
Why is your face so dirty & black
& tattooed where the coal-dust made your skin crack?
You look like you've been to hell & back!
O, Father, we hardly knew ye!

You haven't a future & you haven't a past,
Alas! Alas!
You haven't a future & you haven't a past,
Alas! Alas!
You haven't a future & you haven't a past:
They've both been buried. It happened so fast –
Overruled, undermined, overturned & outclassed –
O, Father, we hardly knew ye!

Sad as it was to see you so,
Boo hoo! Boo hoo!
Sad as it was to see you so,
Boo hoo! Boo hoo!
Sad as it was to see you so,
Singing their *Yes, sir*, dancing their *No*,
It's sadder to see them now letting you go:
O, Father, we hardly knew ye!

> Because now you're a spirit & now you're a ghost,
> & the north wind blows right through ye.
> You drank your life like a river drinks rain:
> Puked it & pissed it away down the drain!
> & now it's too late to complain
> 'O, Father, we hardly knew ye.'

Roy Blackman

'I am not the subject of this sentence'
for Susan Blackmore of The Meme Machine

I am the gene for sterility.
I don't live long.
Aspermia is not passed on.

I am the meme for suicide.
Wherever there are men alive
I thrive.

Ten-to-the-eleven neurons automated in one brain
designated Blackman, Roy. B.Sc. B.A. Ph.D.
This brain has convoluted thoughts.
One of the thoughts it has is me.
Frequently.

Not when absorbed in writing a poem
(except this one, of course)
or any other engrossing chase,
but most of the time:
when I'm dithering, feeling deprived, depressed.

Personality prevents me living.
Become a Buddhist – meditate;
let the brain remain on autopilot.
It knows what it's doing;
knows far more than I

who only gets seduced by memes –
infectious, self-replicating, host-indifferent themes;
the bright ideas that bring me so much pain:
excelling, being in control, saving face,
manhood, cowardice, disgrace.

Each night the ten-point stag searches for his head in the corridors of the archduke's winter palace
in honour of Miroslav Holub

1   There's nothing unusual about losing one's head.

2   It's keeping ahead that's suicidal.

3   As is meeting many things head-on.

4   How can I look for my own head, you're thinking.
    Have you never met anyone off their head before?

5   True, some nights I think it's a mad enterprise,
    like trying to wipe the smile off the Cheshire Cat.

6   Maybe I'm better off without it: my head will never
    be turned again; I'll never fall head-over-heels in love.

7   I'm always in two minds about it: it was a heavy responsibility,
    whereas now my neck is bloody but my head unbowed.

8   Most of us, after all, are frightened of things coming to a head.

9   And what good ever came of letting someone have theirs?

10 But then, it can hardly look for me: stuffed full of rubbish
    and screwed up by fixed ideas.

Watercourse

Aflame with desire,
climbers flash up the braided fuses
to their long set-pieces,
fingers play lovingly over her face,
dislodging grains etched out by rain.
Eaten by lichen, levered by frost,
grit-blasted by storms,
gullies disgorge deltas of dirty sugar.

Grounded by cowardice, I sit
where water-silks cowl and tassel stone,
pour impact at slabs.
Petals jet glass rosettes,
droop gathered curtains,
their fixed ephemeral
dismembering rock.
The resting eye sets flames
to icy flickers.

Past sparging effervescence,
ball-peined bronze,
ripples in the far pool's crucible
trickle light down a twig.
Difficult to persuade the mind
it can't see bright whites
dripping into black.

Hearthside Ease

On the one hand,
brass buckles, a padlock,
button-cleaner, button-hook.

> Hold very tight there; pass right down the bus.
> I had a good home and I left;
> left, left, right, left.

Over and above,
his prized collection
of antique can-openers.

> Punctual, punctilious, punctate, punctured.
> Then rip a jagged thin metal edge
> against your wrists.

On the other, a gasman's
bronze spanner (not to strike a spark)
and iron keys with psychiatric wards.

> 'I have heard the key
> Turn in the door once, and turn once only.'
> One down and none to go. Do; undo.

Closure; disclosure; insecurity.
He's sterile. He walked out on his wife.
His sexual titillation is to

> I am a rock; I am an i-i-island.
> *Esse qua esse bonum est.*
> Never to have been born is best.

Have you ever looked at summer stars
from the middle of your unbuilt, unlit life
after three days of rain have cleared?

Starchild,
my molecules were formed in stars.
Even a star is more than molecules.

The black, billions of light-years deep
and all those tiny pasts, brilliantly burning.
Is there ever an end to it?

I am about to write this sentence.

Lawrence Bradby

VGSOH Essential

Jostled by three-legged puns
I hung up her coat,
then squeezed down the hall
full of wild innuendoes; one slam
and their row was shut out,
our second date begun.

Her gaze calm and intent,
she stepped smartly back
from a delicate joke she'd just built
on my living-room carpet.

Puzzling where she'd found
irony, fuse wire and cocktail sticks
I sneezed, as it turned out,
with far too much force.

What He Gave Me

In the three years he stalled
in the flat above,
Kevin offered me
three house leeks
(ready potted),
the loan of a book
on Chinese regional cuisine,
a masterclass in BASIC,
advice on daffodils,
two bottles of whiskey
(half drunk), a slap,
a game of chess,
Dutch baccy at well below
retail price, his views on why the Saudis
can't be trusted, the numbers of some great lads
in the oil exploration game who'd see me right
if I said his name, a dawn tour
of woods where he suspected ceps
and chanterelles, and constant
assurances that both speakers
were remounted or realigned
and anyway with an output
of only forty milliwatts
I wouldn't be disturbed
again.

I thought I'd accepted none of this,
but even now, years later,
as I shuffle into sleep
what snags and turns me,
calls me back awake,
is an echo of 'Stairway to Heaven',
those gentle opening chords.

A Call to Electricians

Oh, you neat-haired young men
who studied so hard
for your little diplomas,
get in your trim Bedford vans
and come round.
Take your firm hands
from your boilersuit pockets,
glance in my junction box,
let your eyes cloud
as you murmur 'abnormal resistance',
then brightening, 'That's it.
It was only the trip switch.'

But that isn't quite it
for I still have to tell you this story
of minor domestic malfunction
that snakes round my flat like a multiplug
on a long leash, joining
the cooker that hums,
to the hi-fi that crackles
like hot fat,
to much else besides
that needs fixing
please.

Before You Answer

don't forget
that scattered details
give a conversation grip.
So if it's Mum play safe, stay neutral;
mention you've been reading old newspapers,
gathering dustballs, re-alphabetizing your vinyl,
no problem, but keep schtum
about the telescope in the bathroom,
the notes to the milkman,
the salt and the slugs and the toast.

OK, now it's ringing let your heart rate settle

and remember
any twigs of information
dropped before your sister
go straight back to Mum,
so concerning the afternoons leering at traffic,
the project to feed next-door's cat
with last week's failed soufflé,
the millennial twitch (now perfected),
stay buttoned up.

Make the ringing work for you, a reminder

that those few days your brother waited
before he slit the seams on your confidential chat
weren't a lapsed attempt at tact,
but a measure of his laziness
even as a gossip.

That's good, stretch it, leave it just a little longer

then if it's mates
and you're busy peeling rude vegetables,
coining new nicknames
for kids from your old school,
flicking the telly on every sixth minute
to slice across scheduling slots and increase
your chances of finding something bearable,
share what you're doing,
that's fine. They'll sigh and shrug
and condescend a visit
but won't be flaring nostrils,
coughing up the self-improvement quotes
that are provoked by your tales
of spreading jam on stale crusts
whilst reading biscuit wrappers,
visualizing those near to you
held in the purple nurturing glow
from your pyloric sphincter,
the uncertain thrill of wedging yourself
under the sofa, pretending to reach for a tape
and feeling the dustballs
soft as feather boas on your lips.

Now you're ready; you'll be fine; act natural; answer it.

Rumplestiltskin, the King and the Girl

Guess what I first noticed
about you
says one;
make yourself at home
says the other
but remember you're not safe
beyond these four walls.
She sits, apparently listening.

Guess the weight of this cake
to the nearest gram
says one;
make a sandwich into a banquet
says the other.
She keeps counting
down from a thousand.

Guess what the first words
of your first-born will be
says one;
make me feel young again
says the other.
Her jumper sleeves swallow
her fidgeting hands.

Guess where I buried the bones
says one;
make mutton broth
like my mother did
says the other.
She nods her head
again and again.

Guess the name of the vein
that taps above your collarbone
says one;
make it up then
says the other
at least pretend you're having fun.
Her eyeballs skim
under closed lids.

Guess what
says one
you guessed wrong
every time;
please believe
this hurts me more
says the other.

She twists off her ring
hands it to one
cuts off her dry hair with a knife
hands it to the other.

She steps outside without a word
without a thought in the empty street.

Deborah Chivers

Things You Think I Don't Know

You think I don't know
you think that now our darlings are about to leave
our life will expand, flare into technicolour,
Judy-Garland-dazzle us.

You talk of Harley-Davidsons, Spain, galleries, films,
the ocean, the desert, delicious food;
you say: Langoustines! Asparagus! Cream! Cream! Cream!
Like a loving little devil you take me up, up,
and wave your arms about.

You show me books, log fires, Gene Kelly,
things you know me well enough to know I'll want.
All my love, you shout,
hanging on for dear life,
for ever and ever.

You think I don't know
how you stay awake at night
and play a secret tape next to my sleeping ear.
You think I don't know it intones,
please stay, please stay, please stay,
please.

I Picture this Woman

whose middle is squeezed with a wide plaited belt.
She is proud of her slender waist,
and of her bust which now looks quaintly high
and pointed. Ouch! A bloke could lose an eye that way.
Her sweater hugs her angles,
it has a deep plunge at the back,
and no, she is not wearing it the wrong way round.
A fine trail of blond hair follows her spine down.
Give her credit; one baby, and she can still turn heads.
She plucks her eyebrows off, you should hear her sneeze!
Each morning she must pencil in a new pair.
Their shape varies from day to day, depending on her mood.
Some days she draws none at all.

Those vertiginous heels!
Her shoes are plaited too;
woven strips of alternating black and white leather.
Her ankles wobble, and someone says her knees
will pay the price some day.
How can she push her tiny feet into the witchy points?
Where did she get those crazy shoes?
She wears a dirndl skirt;
see the way it flares out
from her waist of which she is a little vain.
Her hips are narrow too;
they don't affect the skirt's mad line at all.
It seems she wears a hundred net petticoats.

She loves the white-coated chemist-ladies,
their dainty hands and cloppy heels,
unlikely coloured hairdos.
Can I help you, they murmur, and show her
how makeup looks on the insides of their pale wrists.
They gather round her in the air
that smells of Germolene and Blue Grass,
offering sniffs of Evening In Paris.
She can't imagine them ever frying sausages!
No one expects them to provide a greaseproof-paper packet
of cheese and brown sauce sandwiches every day.
She buys her lipsticks,
borrowing from the rent money:
Tender Touch, Dusky Pout, French Kiss.

Heron

I had this long dream
smelling of frog-spawn.
It was full of feathers
that brushed my bare shoulders
like warm ferns,
and thin, funnily-hinged legs;
I had a feeling of being trampled.
There was a snaky shape
always weaving about.
I kept seeing shining, flat eyes.

Eventually I made it to morning,
stretched my arms, yawned,
and saw a heron
sitting in the wide-open bedroom window.
Its compact head
pushed the curtain to one side,
its neck described a question mark.
Webbed feet, the colour of old egg-yolks,

hung down in rubbery folds
against the radiator.
Giving me one serious look,
then pivoting its head outwards,
he launched off inelegantly.
Breast feathers like flakes of new sky
floated onto the carpet.
A breeze blew in from the river
and lifted my fringe.

Then I noticed:
on my husband's side of the bed,
in a nest of ripped pillows,
sat a huge, pale blue egg.
I put my ear to the still-warm smoothness
and heard a knocking sound,
someone calling my name.
A piece of shell fell on the duvet.
I put my eye to the chink.
Darling? I said.

Clare Crossman

Home Life

If anyone had told her that
it might be of interest,
she never would have started.
Twelve chapters taped along the back,
and a file of photographs.
Her, and Jim, with friends
at the club in Kenya.
Gin, cane furniture and bracelets,
the other wives wanting to come home.

She sifts her memory,
for glimpses of the past.
Those things that make her
who she is at eighty.
It seems they lived in Albert Villas recently,
the schoolroom, the piano,
the ferns in the conservatory.
She feels closer to her mother now,
wears out of habit, her seed pearls.

When they came back to England
she kept a diary: new ideas for easy meals,
how to appliqué a cushion.
Descriptions of neighbours known
only superficially.
The realization that she might always live
in a suburban road and never be
an expert on the crystal stones,
she loved along the coast of Ireland.

'It's for my daughter and the children.
All this, of course,
a vanished way of life.'
Home life, a journal of interiors
full of people never really talking.
Her hands move surely across the paper,
writing slowly, at the same table where
she paid the bills and wept.
A woman overlooking a long garden,
pushing against silence,
arguing with rain.

Going Back

It's always a sentimental journey,
especially at the river. I imagine
I could sail down between the
warehouses and the boats
and we would still be there:
my brother and myself, in
the square Edwardian house,
sycamore wings falling, on Laburnum Avenue.

We flew kites high above the
wasteground, biked home
past the evening traffic.
I am reminded of museums on
wet afternoons. The armchair
in the attic, the tent we slept
in on the lawn, when the heat
in summer sent us wishing for storms.

It's an old map.
I keep it carefully, in a secret
place; retrace its charts and routes,
the dog we had, the nature trail,
the rusty shed where we
invented journeys we might
take on trains that rumbled underground.

What I might have been is in the dust
of pavements, this steamed up café,
familiar places on the *A–Z*.
My mother has fallen asleep
over a book. My father, outside,
is digging greenness into the lawn.
We are climbing, to look out across gardens
into long hours of August and the moon.

The Sisters

The sisters used to go out dancing,
in rock and roll outfits they had designed
themselves. They waited at tables, took
orders, delivered drinks, to save for
foreign travel, and made Grace Kelly
entrances in billowing circular skirts.

Their friends called round to swop ideas.
Brothers and friends of brothers
drove up in clapped out cars.
These were evenings on the wild side,
shared beers and cigarettes, a time
to dream a world where love was best.

The sisters learned the village
children's names. Taught difficult boys
who only played guitars. Filled their
front room with adopted nieces.
Walked the canal bank when work was finished
and took in pitmen's widows washing.

The sisters moved away to cities,
put the old house up for sale.
When they had gone there was
a silence in the street, nowhere to
talk something difficult over,
only the corner shop in which to meet.

Weekend People

On Friday I see them coming back
just as the evening is beginning
and the streets are full of the rush for home.
Doors slam, and there are voices in the garden,
someone plays the piano slowly until late.

During the week the house sits vacant,
almost waiting.
Old garden chairs left upturned,
the water barrel seeping.
Nothing that will damage in the rain.

Late at night sometimes I think I hear a flute,
as if someone had stayed behind,
unable to let go of the weather.
The gutters gurgle and drain. And
the gate is swinging.

They are putting something aside,
my neighbours, in this windswept town.
Our uncurtained windows are still lives,
plants and lampshades, a cracked flowerpot,
a candelabra burning.

At night the only sound is
the roar of motorbikes at midnight,
arcing into the next valley.
We keep our distance, and look up.
The spaces and the trees between us, greening.

The Field

The field has never been cut.
He drives past it every day,
waits for those afternoons in June,
when it is full of fritillary, and eyebright,
bugle and buttercups:
flowers that have seeded themselves,
blown in from the road.
He thinks he should keep a diary,
become an amateur naturalist,
note the date of the first star flower,
and when the rosebay signals that
the year is turning to
dewed webs in the grass.
Privately he calls it the burning field.
It seems to flicker every golden colour
and he could paint it from memory.

He trespasses with his children regularly.
Emerging from the wood at the bottom,
they lie down amongst the couch-grass heads,
that point to heaven, and wait to
feel the earth turning.
Amongst buildings and in cities,
he returns to the endless blue
they've seen above their heads.
The way the field waits under snow
and then suddenly is full of ladybirds and green.
The field stays with him,
a wild meadow, always returning summer.
Where his daughter chases butterflies
and grass seed drops in sandwiches,
and he lies head to head with his son,
pretending to be Indians.
He thinks that paradise might be like that.

David Evans

Thread

I know why myths and fairytales
of the thread
strike such a chord,
think of it:

the Ariadne that goes with you
in every decision you make.

The tortuous convolution
of every desire or drive
leaves a trace.

All that's left
is a pink line to your heart,

and only you know
how you got there,
only you know how to get out.

Frogs

It is akin to draining
the marshes
in its effect.
Yes, it is cleansing. Also it is

sucking the blood from my lips:
my stomach falters,
my legs swim on dry land,
heartbeats, like frogs,

leave the place that poisons them.

Ghost Train

Last night, sleeplessly, I dreamt
how much like a ghost train
sleeping is. The same kind
of uncertainty heading out,

the same median at which
the outward journey
becomes the return trip.
Along the ride I half recognize faces.

My sister: The Palace of Swords.
A lover: The House of Wax.

The places where
the train makes as if to ram a wall
dissolving in a pull
of curtains drawing back.

Ivy Garlitz

Mitochondria
after Bertolt Brecht

I, Cheya Fagel, was pushed to the palm trees
from the tenements inside my mother.
And the dank coldness of the tenements
will stick inside me until my dying day.

Though I was rocked by the lulling Atlantic
and from the start was given every sacrament
I felt within the villas and mast antennae
the creaking staircases, pitched halls and the wind;

like my mother, shipped to the asphalt city
from the wooden lean-tos and brick milkvahs
inside my grandmother, her muddied sheds,
can still hear wolves howling in snow, lashed horses;

and my grandmother, whose name I bear,
and was swaddled to the frozen Vistula,
inside my great-grandmother could remember
the desert, fire and wandering.

And somewhere, the woman who first carried my name
was cradled to that desert and the tents
from the mountain in her mother's body
and the long night of waiting by its pinnacle.

In the earthquakes that will come, I hope
to sense the mountain passed down to me, enwrapped
in the desert, the river, the trampled fields,
the streets that ran in my mother, choked with broken glass.

Losing You

is like running down to the harbour
to see the ship I've awaited all my life
pulling away, the passengers, you, waving,
celebrating their departure and themselves
with raised champagne, the lights blazing,
the orchestra playing happy love songs,
streamers falling in the waves,
tugs following in the churning wake,
while I stand helplessly,
pressing against the barrier on the pier,
staring at the upturned gangway,

watching my ship – you – disappear
without me, the life I might have had,
hoped to have, fading in each blast
of the horn, growing more and more distant.
It does not console me remembering
that when Jerome Kern, the composer of our song,
at the beginning of his career woke up too late,
rushed to the docks and watched
his liner with his promised producer
set sail without him, leaving him behind,
his ship was the *Lusitania*.

The Lighter Side
after Dave Berg

Roger Kaputnik, a family man
from the first, with properly crewed hair,
ribbon-slim tie, apples in his intray,
gnawed cores in the out,
mounted tranquillizer dispenser

aside his name spelled out on the frosted door.
At home, his wife in ruffled pinafore
urges the two tinies, full of Good Humor,
to eat the dinners she lovingly defrosted.
Kaputnik, in short-sleeved buttoned leisurewear,

points away from the TV, biting his pipe,
his black frames slipping down his nose.
In his fedora, his belted raincoat, loafers,
he shouts at the clipped newspaper, grabs his case,
while his aproned wife calls from the kitchen

the girl and boy have current events.
She waits for them to drive home from dates,
to eschew the miniskirts, the beards,
their Ivy League friends in cut-offs,
their protest circles, their mandalas,

to found their own split-level.
She pushes the vacuum in the empty house,
slippered and rollered, one eye still on the set;
Kaputnik, gone grey from his sideburns up,
sits on the table in his undershirt

baring his teeth on his corncob pipe.
The doctor, with mirror perched
above his squared off eyes,
is ready to spend twenty years
relaying the results,

causing Kaputnik to cry to God
repeatedly,
only the gag line altered.

Hannah Godfrey

Gauloises

I could go out for cigarettes
one afternoon
and never come back;

discard my heels for daughter's trainers,
swop my slacks for a flaming sarong:
a skirt, a veil, an invitation
easily undone.

I'd let strangers buy me coffee,
give me lights, touch my face;
my regrets would be few and sweet,
unimportant and my own.

I could go out for cigarettes
one afternoon
and never come back.

Avenue Hill

Down Avenue Hill the houses curve like vertebrae;
I haven't seen your spine
but can't help imagining it whenever I pass.

Further along, the sun draws the trees' fingers
across the road,
their leaves' tart colour
deepening with the evening.

Stars prickle an uncomplicated blackness.
The air is crisp.
A cyclist passes, a body of messages.

The Cocoon Café

Like moths weary of the city's bright lights
tired men and women hoping to escape
enter the rain-dimmed café
to order cocoa and cake.

As they settle the lamps are darkened,
cups and plates are pushed away
as heads are lain,
glazed eyes closed,
and limbs curled.

Somnambically methodical, the waiters become keepers
and gently slip each dormant form into downy sacks,
they hoist them up, without a sound, into the cosy rafters
where lights lie buried, soft and soft
lullabies to such workers.

Mark Haddon

Physics

In 4B Mr Manning sketched the atom
as a microscopic solar system,
electrons spinning round the nucleus
like planets orbiting the sun,
which made me wonder whether all the atoms
in a dinner plate were tiny stars
and underneath my pears and custard
on the surface of some smaller Earth
a freakish, shrunken replica of me
was looking at the pears and custard
on his plate and wondering.
The universes in their billions,
nested like a set of Russian dolls.

In 6A Mrs Jordan said that atoms
didn't *look like* anything, light being
far too coarse a brush to paint that small.
That Mr Manning's solar system sketch
was only an illuminating lie
and we could no more see the stuff we're made of
than the smell of rain, or no tomatoes,
or the thoughts inside another mind.

Now, when I read how everything
exploded from a lump of matter
smaller than a human head
I think of science as a kind of poetry,
that original illuminating lie
which joined the dots between the stars,
and read the shapes as characters
in stories of a world too fine
for human eyes and ordinary light.
And sometimes I can almost see the smell of rain.

Louse Point

He rarely paints these days.
Mostly he just stands and looks
at half-completed canvases,
turning every now and then
to rinse his eyes in the ocean light
which filters through the scrub oaks
and pours into the high, white room,
waiting for that rare ecstasy
when the mind gutters out
but the hand still moves
and makes a mark that shocks him
with the rightness of a long-forgotten answer.

But the answers come less often now.
He is an old man
and the waiting and the looking
have themselves become the work,
a kind of silent prayer
in which the heart learns how to let go.

He dreams of painting one last masterpiece,
an image like the image of his liver-dappled hands,
or like the branches on the far side of the glass,
more found than made, hardly a picture,
so the eye no longer searches but is bathed
in browns and oranges and blues
in curves and in corners,
as his mind bathes in the books
he reads each night before he sleeps,
not for language or for character or plot
but for deliverance from this room,
from this body and from this failing light.

Midas

When everything inside the palace
had been turned to gold – the queen
howling silently for ever
at his clutch, grapes like a nest
of earrings, every yellow surface
decorated with his own face
twisted out of shape and crawling
with the shiny beetles of his tears –
he reached out and touched this page
and turned a story all of us
should take to heart about the way
greed kills the things we love
into a golden heirloom
every generation hands down
to the next, priceless,
perfectly preserved and dead.

But rub the tarnish off and turn
the pages back to find the prologue
where the king-to-be is lying
in his wicker crib and, marching
back and forth between the pillow
and the window ledge,
an endless chain of ants
is feeding him with grains of wheat,
the meaning of the story
still unwrapped, the image fresh
as water poured into a clay jug
or a hot loaf not yet frozen
by the king's rage to possess.

Flying to Minneapolis

The fear starts with the flash and crack
of lightning out beyond the runways
and the big jets kicking in. I close my eyes
and shrink to something small and hard
inside my chest and count the seconds
of the grinding climb through blue explosions
till at last the storm dies and I look down.
Half a mile below the fuselage
New York flows like lava,
the black rind cracked
by oozing freeways of tangerine light.
And I'm not frightened any more.

This is the dream we've dreamt
for fifty thousand years.
I'm wearing Ten League Boots.
I'm Daedalus and Peter Pan.
I'm the light ghost of Troilus
gazing down upon this *litel spot of erthe*
that with the see embracéd is,
the sectored fields of Pennsylvania,
Scranton, DuBois, Cleveland
and the moon flaring on Lake Erie.

I sleep, soothed by the engines'
thundering lullaby and wake to find us
swimming down through turquoise cloud
into the clear, deep air
above the rockpool glitter
of the Twin Cities.

Now, when I think of dying,
this is how I try to picture it.
The mind crying out for help
and nothing I can do but wait
and trust that with the growing distance
comes one last, clear view,
that same solving wonder,
then the final sleep
above the weather's changes,
and no waking.

New Year's Day

The knife-cold of the remade year.
Down the road across the salt marsh,
over the clack and slip
of the shore's pebbled barrow
and into the boom of surf.
Wet stone, white air and rocking water.
I find a strand of powdered shell
and run into my breath for three miles
to the spur's blunt head
until there's nowhere else to go,

then stand and watch
where, every year,
a little of the ocean
slows and falls
and turns into a yard of land.

And at a vaguer edge
where something of the emptiness
we spin through silts and settles
so that we can walk, each year,
a little further out into the fog.

Danny Hardisty

A Walk Down

It was a final walk
alongside white painted fences:
the scrap of a wall
and an iron bridge, rivets
like huge buttons.

Mine was a small hand
in a big palm – watching flashes of trees:
willows, stitches of bud.
Then between the fence lines
the shape of sunlight full
on grass – swimming like water.

Images that could fit
any story – that could
happen next. The fence;
the bridge; the mirage
of sunlight on dew grass –
I can't remember the rest.

You'd think they'd stay
these moments, importantly –
one boy's walk with a father
who would go for good
after. But they don't,
they ripen, falling

leaving that space
where they were once –
and the places they happened.
A blank above a hand
and the line of a white fence.

Say Something

Glasses are poured and rush to edges,
fizz settling back from the rim –
trays and plates taken and thank-you'd,
or passed on down the table.

The silence that settles again starts
to seem certain, after each commotion
of more this or that – crackers snapped,
I'm not sure how things are supposed to be spoken.

My sister is eight years old and knows
to be quiet when nothing's to be said.
The sink of her serious lips,
the stillness of effort behind her eyes

say something.

A Wedding Ceremony

A hall in white. People turning to food
at the back. If this were a film we'd catch
the cut-aways now, shots we didn't get
during the ceremony – the close-up
of candle flames, a nerve-edged word.

We might capture the crowd looking down before
they sit, the voice reading a poem in front
of where you two stand. The way words were said
bracketed outside a frame that didn't
fit two faces – a truth of it. This footage:

your palm clasping your dead father's watch,
acting anxiety for the camera –
Where's the bride? Closer: small numbers,
and the grass twitch of a second-hand.
Stitches of a chain couple it to your jacket.

Ramona Herdman

Slur

Yeah, fair enough carousing, fair enough
the drugs – I know that 'fun' can't do them justice.
And fair as hell, the early hours, I know.
They're fine as lovers' hair, they flare like laughs
in conversation, fire against the night.
I don't want to deny you absconding, don't want
you catching pleasures in flight, roses ripped
while ye may. Define 'joy'. Define 'fright'.
Now divide by the result. Don't flinch.
Don't reach for the panacea of the thrill,
the easy chemical. I like you high.
But I like you sober as well. Don't tell
me you could stop if you wanted to. Why
don't you want to? What's there to feel?

Twelfth Night: Maria

The Rules say Never Call
but what if he lives in the same
Great House as you?
What if you hold a begging bowl
up to his hangovers,
fill his cup and wipe the lip
free of the red lick of wine?
What if, once or twice,
it's he who calls you
to his bedside,
turns over with eyes like owl-holes,
opens and fumbles the red baby shrew of his cock
into your hand and looks up, eyes shut
in the crook of your shoulder and breast
and breathes 'Yes' eyes shut
like the suck of a babe
at your abandoned breast?
What if he rests a hand
occasionally on the ache
of the small of your back
at work, the other hand
waltzing a bottle?
What have I lost
always looking to see if he looks?
I despise myself
for walking the ways he might be,
seeking the mistake
of him bumping into me.

The Ballad of

He had his head hit
twenty-eight times in the slam
of the door of the van
of a mate.

His head was one
of those lightly overbalancing ones
in primary school,
pale and sable, unstable,
too soft to touch.
He had to sit
at the front, restricted, quieted,
at the level of the teacher's wrist.

He was ahead
of the easier rest of us,
was one of the first
getting pissed in the streets.
One of the worst
of the boys, one of the last
you'd want on your bus.
He troubled. Fussed.
Was all mistrust, grinning.
One of the boys who won't win,
who, long run, obvious,
easy guess, will end up, at least
last, addicted, socially tiresome
financially distressed.

He was battered till his brain leaked
into the mud.
I never saw the blood.
Should have seen it coming.
He was always the last one running after the taunt.
The one caught.
As though that was all there was to want.

He only almost died,
and everyone, everyone
matronly wishes that he had,
that he would
for his sake, for the sake of his mother, mopping
his drool, for his sake, waking
to the wreck of flesh
tangled like a jellyfish hanging off his neck
but mostly for us, for our sake, for the sake
of our escape from the thought of him.

His life isn't over.
The evening paper campaigned for his wheelchair.
He makes a photo-feature in the stands of every Stoke game.
His hands are too crumpled in newsprint to see
but I want them to be
obscene, all tooth and nail and drug deal
like they used to be.
To hold what he used to have –
his shoplifting, his lust
for trouble, of getting kicked off,
of the chance to hit first.

I forget him
as often as I can.
If these are wars,
and I think they are, I think they have been made.
I think if you're small
enough they always are, for he and I
they were, then I was born
to a backroom corps
and he to untelevised places, messy with bombs.

He was one of the ones
not to touch with a bayonet
for fear of what you'd get
even before he was mangled, before
he had to be unpicked, unrolled with a boot
to find out if he were dead.
He always stunk of blood,
fierce as prey.

Take him away.

I am more scared of him, the more crippled he gets.
He is not dead yet,
lest I forget.

Yannick Hill

The Portrait

Her breathing is difficult. I wait for my grandmother
On the steps. She looks at me, and her face
Is luminous, like light in a dream.
She breathes as if the air were painted in a picture;
As if she were painting, choosing the right colour.
I stop on the same steps as her on our way home.

She says I should consider her house my home.
I hold her hand, and soon my grandmother
Is breathing the air as if dreaming in colour.
She lets go of my hand and touches my face.
She says she will paint me in a picture.
I tell her she appeared in my last dream.

She asks me if she can paint my next dream.
She sleeps. The sun listens at the walls of her home,
Presses on her skin, on the canvas of her picture
Of my last dream. I sleep. My grandmother
Wakes during the night, her face
Tender with dreaming. The colour

Of her hair in the dark is like the colour
Of rain falling in a dream,
Collecting in streams that press gently round her face.
She says one day rain will fall in her home,
Because of all the tears she has not cried. My grandmother
Decides to have rain fall in a painted picture.

Today my grandmother took a picture
Of our family together. She made sure it was a colour
Film. Her yellow tablecloth out especially. My grandmother
Says that last night she had a dream
About sunlight shining through the walls of her home.
She says she still feels it like a fever on her face.

I hold her hand and touch her face
With my other hand. She says her picture
Of me is finished. She will hang it in her home.
She had difficulty finding the right colour
For my eyes. She found the colour in a dream.
I take a photograph of my grandmother.

She covers her face with her hands to hide the colour
Of her eyes. Her picture of my last dream
Also hangs in her home. It is a painting of rain falling on my
grandmother.

The Planetarium

When it was cold outside,
We went to the planetarium,
Mother and son,
Where they stitch together evenings,
Like seamsters of an air balloon.

Inside, a night sky,
A room, warm
As an aquarium;
A projector, a sea urchin,
Floating above us.

A phosphorescence of cold stars
Moves across our hemisphere,
Like a film
About sunlight
On the tops of waves.

In the planetarium,
I listened to you in the dark,
And the stars did not wink.
There, we could talk, son and mother,
Outside, it hurt to smile;

No light to distract you
From my tone of voice;
No eyes for you
To make sense
Of my mouth.

After the planetarium,
I began to sew my own balloon,
To fly over waves
And see the stars
Move across our hemisphere.

The Test
at Holkham Beach

I had to cross
A fever of red samphire,
A field like the underside of anger,
To be surrounded by sand,
By a sadness
You prepared me for
When you lived across a sea,
Away from me.

The sea dies beautifully
On this beach.
Waves lay themselves to rest
In the laps of a shoreline.
I use razor shells to cut
New journeys for the backwash,
To delay your leaving,
As if the tide were grieving.

The pines that keep
The secrets from the beach,
Are where I might
Have hidden from you;
Never long enough
To really test you.
I will today stay in a tree,
To see if you are missing me.

Andrea C Holland

I'm Looking at a Sunflower, Lopsided

in a full field of sunflowers. Each
one is a part of the overall plan
of sunflowers. Each one is a seed

in a field full of seeds,
like the skull of black seeds on each
sunflower head. I'm looking

at yellow, and at the wrap of blue
that is sky above each stem. The cape
of shadow over every one.

I'm looking at a painting by Egon Schiele
and there are no people in it,
and I realize that in paintings

by Egon Schiele, which feature people,
he paints women like awkward birds
among slight stalks of full sunflowers,

in a lopsided field. (His wife is a pigeon,
his sister is a crow, all black skull
and lopsided eye, like a seed.)

That is how close I am.

Cloud Cover

Misty cobwebs break over your face
as you step out the back door, breathing
in. It feels like the shivers, someone

just walked on your grave. Your breath
goes through the web and then your skin.
Getting out is what counts. All week you read

about a dead woman's life, how it ended
in the kitchen. Your own tea towels and tubs
of rice seem to be conspiring: watch out

for the crude corer, the big knife's steel grin.
(They mock, *if you can't stand the heat get out
of the kitchen/ Gas! Gas! Quick boys! – an ecstacy*

of fumbling). For seven days you wondered
how it would finish up though you knew,
you always knew how the pages stop turning,

how the heart stops. But in the end, revelation,
(mist on your face), the gas bill for February
forwarded to Devon, to Sylvia's tenant:

You were her friend. You pay the bill.

Andrea C Holland

Self-Burial, 1969
from a photograph by Keith Arnatt

I was led here, it's true. But I am willing.
Each day I am muddled into the earth,
disappearing like a bombed out city,
like Dresden. It's important you see me
go like this: I've come here to let go
of gravity – my feet are tired like donkeys
at the beach; always the endless back
and forth. The weight of the body.
In winter, in places too cold to stand,
wild horses lie deep in the snow:
they go down into the drifts, become
invisible and stay warm. I look also
to moles, earthworms, the hare
and the fox. I see rabbits go down
into the good earth. I don't eat. I want
for nothing.

I am leaving behind a scar on the land,
a scratch of soil, but you'll find no
reminder. This is not semaphore,
or loss. There's nothing left to say.
You have to let me go.

Return Home by Weeping-Cross

*To return home by weeping-cross. . . to repent sorrowfully having taken
a certain course.* (Dictionary of the English Language, *1897)*

Summer stacked in raw fields – that is straw.
It is blond, dry, animal food.
Straw towers wrapped in black plastic,
like a roof, for protection.
And yet look how hay houses are rained into ruin.

So then you build with sticks, which are not worth much
more than straw. What good but in the burning?
And, here, I burnt other things besides – spindly kindling
the least best thing. I burnt my mouth. You, by
degrees.

And so to bricks. Red bricks as bold as love.
Who needs timber, with all its hesitation
and rot? Bricks, mortar – of these a home
is made. We go inside to be warm. We go
out and forget the key. But that is not
where I went wrong: I blew down every house
you built. I return home, lupine, each night
by weeping-cross.

Matthew Hollis

And

Everything will be all right I know,
though nothing feels less certain now, less sure.
Some things we keep some things we just let go.

So many things seem far outside the flow
of our control that this is just one more;
and everything will be all right I know.

These things I cannot stop or even slow,
the fear there's nothing to be done, that you're
one more thing I cannot keep, – one more thing let go.

Bad news, at times, will lay out in a row,
with nothing held together anymore;
but everything will be all right I know.

If I could change a thing I would do so,
put back the clocks, retrace my steps on every floor:
no, we cannot keep all things, some let us go.

From everything comes something else. And though
it may be less, be lesser than before,
everything will be all right I know.
Some things we keep some things we just let go.

Harwonder
for C

Perhaps it was the way we caddied the sound,
or delighted at its invention.

But more likely it was the sharing of a word
that no-one else knew –

a language for two, putting a name
to what we have between us –

'harwonder', a term of no strict definition,
but intimately ours –

                musical, made up of us;
where language was a kind of touch, a pull

as inevitable as any vinyl's concentric,
a groove we could not depart from.

And even before you spoke of being
unable to fight it any more

I had long since given myself up to you
and your perfect pitch.

And you lead me through, and into you,
to feel a slow crescendo;

and all and two-thirds of the world
was tuning-up beneath our feet

converging on a single note.

Blink

as your eye closes (slowly
like canopy lowering to rain,
or wing touching a far floor,
shedding a slightest, most fragile tear,
the shape of wave, the shape of breaker, un-
breaking across a round sea, to somewhere
shore, where am I stood and, seeing, find
in you I hope, my reflection,
unmistakably, in your paper-
weight look, in your closed
eye) and opens

Wake

That dream again – you hadn't stayed
but crossed a life from side to side
and painted out its picture. I start,
and cast the darkness for sense.
But the clock-light is runic,
and the shadows will not realize,
and I would not wake you to check you here;
though I do not hear you breathe,
or feel your touch, you have not gone.
We have simply turned aside to sleep.

Helen Ivory

The Cows in My Garden Swim in Moonlight

in paths mapped out by the stars.
They move in single file,
slow silhouettes in the moonlit dark.
Their breath warms the air in clouds
and low music fills the air,
tugging at the edges of my dreams.
I breathe in the scent of their skin
and see the stars reflected in their eyes.

We are navigated to pastures
that sing with the sounds of the night.
I stand still as the cows pass me by.
They are silent now, and seem to move as one,
padding softly in the long grass,
dissolving in the space between night and day.
And all day the stars are blinded by the sun.

The Sky Wolf

That night the moon came up as usual.
Nocturnal creatures made
their customary music,
and people closed their curtains
and lit their lamps and fires.

The wolf that chases the sun
had made good ground for once;
with one snap of his awesome jaw
he swallowed it whole,
singeing his fur a little in the process.

By day the moon was a distant ghost
in the still, dark sky,
and people lit their lamps again
and tried to go about their business.
The day was long and as cold as night.

As night fell, the moon lit up the land
and they walked outside
just to bathe in its light.
Owls swooped overhead by day
and flowers pressed their petals shut.

The wolf was pursuing the moon by now,
snapping at its aura.
People watched and feared the worst;
crowding together on hills and mountains,
appealing to the gods for mercy.

All at once a spear of lightning
ripped the wolf from tail to snout.
His blood rained down in fire and ash,
filling the seas and drowning the land.
And then there was dark and silence.

Later, dawn broke across the world.
The last remaining tree
held its leaves to the sun. The birds
and creatures that were sheltering there
walked in the light once more.

And in the sky a wolf uncurled,
hungrily scanning the stars

The Weight of a Hundred Babies

When, like a ravening wolf,
fire ate everything in sight, turning crops
into charcoal and air into poison,
all the pregnant women of the land
gave birth to fireflies.

And in their thousands
these tiny amber lights
danced above the burning towns,
moving higher and higher
till there was no smoke to dull them.

The women wrung their hands in grief
as they watched their children
soar far out of sight;
they knew they were lost for ever
to the star-spattered sky.

Years passed and the land became dead;
no crops would grow
in the blackened earth,
and no children were born.
People grew older and sadder.

Then one day a miracle;
it began to rain.
Every drop was huge,
like a giant bubble reflecting colours
of the time before fire.

Wherever a drop landed,
a tree or a clump of grass
or a flower sprung from the ground.
If it fell in the arms of a woman,
it became a new baby smelling of dew.

The women blessed the sun
and the stars and the moon
as they juggled the babies in their arms,
crushed by the weight
of the hundreds they were trying to catch.

Jessica Jacobs

the carpenter's call to Dali's girl with curls

With the soft sole of your exposed
right foot Where are you Who
are you   the line of your back and the languid stream
of gilded hair Your head is bent
listening What music have you been given

Though you are only
oil on panel painted so thin
the grain shows through
Though your sky is pocked
by unsmoothed wood your soil
in turmoil from knots though your land
is less like land and more like
the sea   I long for you
Hang you above my bed

one nail and you are mine

this is why

I was the only young person
asked *ton* Bobbi and the car full
of old people touring for a week
the coast of Normandy

I was fourteen and this was my summer
in Paris   Omaha they coaxed
the battlefields   *Pointe du Hoc* Juno
beach *Coleulle-sur-mer* fields
of white crosses three hundred and seven
unknown soldiers   But I was fourteen
and this was my summer
in *Chateau d'Ile* the house
of the island This was my summer
my final week I said no

I think of this now
because you hold out your hand

Because now I know I should have gone
with the four of them who played
cards in the evenings and
taught me the French
names of the berries we baked

I think of this now as you hold out
your hand and ask me to grow
old with you I think of this I say yes

hesitance

I

Ondaatje tells of these first pure notes.
The musician's refuge in the long
introduction, his hesitance to enter
the body of the song. Captivated
by what he has found so quickly. Wise
to know it will not last. He sounds
this wisdom thoroughly. Lingers
in the doorway, looking in.

The structure is perfect only so long
as he does not enter it.

2

In these nights before my leaving, you
curl upon my chest, trusting me
with the sweet burden of your body.
I struggle against sleep, wanting to remember
everything: this is the sound of a woman's
heels, tripping the cobblestones in the alley below.
This is the way my mouth fits to your eyelid.
Your cheek is salty with the heat of our bedroom.

These are the things I will lose with the morning.

3

Knowing we will not see each other
for many months, or longer, we make love
with a hunger that looks like cruelty.

On the train, days later, I finger the bruises
fading from my shoulder, the long scratch
healing beneath my ribs. I close my eyes
against the relentless motion of the train.
Trying to remember the warm smell of your hair.
The graceful song of your body.

Christopher James

The Swimmer

Those are her fingertips
there on the page,

where she marked her place
with a fold.

You can barely make them out:
the concentric swirls, in their
                fragile orbits.

The trace is so faint
they are almost imaginings,

but there they are,
printed in oil and brine

and besides, trapped in the spine,
is a spindle of sand,

salt and pepper shards of quartz
refracting ten different colours
                at once.

It defies a shaking.

And then, where the edge curls
like an emergent wave,

I can hear it now,
there is the tiny rip,

produced, by her startled hand,
when she saw the figure rise

streaming,
from the silver plane of the sea.

The Nightwatchman

He watches the skies
with eyes like the bloodshot moons of ruined frescoes.
His hair is smeared like black treacle across his scalp.
       Under this fortieth night of rain,
his cape is as taut and bright as the shell of a dung beetle.
Ponte Vecchio. The bridge sags with shops. They hang
       like saddlebags over the water.
A petroleum torch is extinguished by a rain-gust,
as easily as a candle flame, pinched
       between a damp finger and thumb.
       The river is churned by an unseen hand;
it will move sideways through the city rising
as the Madonna in a foaming plume outside
the doors of the cathedral.
       He does not wake them yet.
Only when the bridge begins to shake
and the wind sings to the song of a collapsing camber
       will he scuttle to their doors.
Then he watches from the shadows:
       the perfumier clearing his display,
filling his pockets with jars of jasmine and juniper,
       dousing his shirt with what he cannot carry.

He watches the shopkeepers observe their strange code
and wait – while the jeweller, delayed by his slight limp,
plucks the solid gold hands from the face of a clock.
    They do not speak to each other;
not even when dawn breaks and Florence is in flood
    and the ghost of Pier della Vigna silently
plunges through a lilac sky from the tower of Rocca,
a stone still pressed into the cold pit of his palm.
    On the riverbed a wound clock without hands
chimes an unknown hour.

The Discovery of Thin Air

Extending a hand
to spoon myself slowly out of bed,

I had forgotten
the outcome of last night's bet:

the settling of spinning silver,
that had given me the top bunk,

a taste of the high life and a licence
finally to rule the skies.

But this reminder of thin air;
the calm drop, the curious snap

and swerve of my arm
and the white springing

of my brother's eyes,
brings rushing back

the final listing of the coin
on my father's wrist

and the wet prism of his face
in the doorway:

*he had better have broken
his arm for this.*

James Knox Whittet

After Dark

In a small Highland town, a Free Church elder would only take his brain damaged son out under cover of darkness.

He takes you out for an airing after dark
when rain slackens its hold on the river,
past the chained swings that hang limp in the park
where the reflections of plane trees shiver
across the heightened pond. Joined by the hand,
you move together past the lighted lives
of others, climbing the brae, leaving the town:
its talking behind backs; words scarring like knives;
the stares of strangers, night streets that lamps strand;
stepping on narrow, strawed farm roads that drown

the echoes of motion. Night after night,
you follow in the footsteps of father's shame;
revealed by a late car's unforgiving light,
he turns his head, unable to confront the blame.
You struggle to speak but no words can be traced:
language defeats you so you hit out in anger,
your free hand flailing at nothing in the dark.
You disturb puddles where diesel strands linger,
then some drowning, distorted stranger's face
looms up at you, mocking your cries when dogs bark

from the still-lit, uncurtained bay window
that glares down on the lawn where elm branches
move shadows in the night sky's mysterious glow
before morning lights the wings of chaffinches
showering themselves in shallow pools that streams
recycle. You pass the churchyard by the bridge
where the dead are kept behind walls in rows
for ease of counting. Birches form a ridge
along the river whose sounds flow into your dreams
and you begin to falter as its motion slows

until sudden, scented winds brush back your hair
and an owl measures night's depths with its call
in those remembered moments you can share
when your hands weld and your separate steps fall
as one on moss that joins fractured pavements;
remaining awake while unknowing others sleep,
listening to sounds only night can bring,
running fingers across daylight's undersides;
held and kept afloat beyond words' currents
where silence and darkness merge in waves to sing.

The Descent

They find him hanging
from a rafter
in the barn,
his tongue blackened
and protruding
in contempt of life
but his toes
stretch towards
the log pile
as if he'd
changed his mind:
too late.

Orange binder twine,
a little frayed,
grips his lengthened neck
as it grips the straw
head of a scarecrow
swollen on a rake
shaft, keeping wood pigeons
off the kale
in that unsteady,
early light
sea gives off.
His dungarees,
patched with cow dung,
bulge at the crotch
with its dried,
off-white stains
that would never
be removed.
His rigid body
sways in the breeze,
scented with neeps,
the way it swayed
standing on the swing
as a child,
rising between elms,
their branches
taking the strain,
complaining
only a little
as the wet rope bruised
their seeping bark
in shafted sunlight
that penetrated
their translucent leaves.
Standing tall
and ascending,
head and shoulders

above them all,
gazing across
the Sound of Islay
at those fires
of heather
blackening slopes of Jura:
strands of smoke
lolling and thinning
as they rose
into spring air
when gorse
throws out
yellow petals
to light the moor.

His uncle, arms raised,
saws through the stranded
twine with a blunted
pruning knife,
then the father
takes hold
of his son
when he
descends
to his
level.

A Brief History of Devotion

They pack auditoriums to hear you,
worshippers of the loose-limbed oracle
whose electric voice reverberates
through those vast interstices where God hides.
Out of the black hole of the stage's wing,
you glide silently and effortlessly
on oiled wheels: a warrior bruised by stars;
your screened dictionary of revealed truths
mounted on technology's chariot:
wisdom's dark matter spread and lit before you.

Pilgrims applaud beneath your lifted feet,
brushed by particles of light reflected
from your highlighted singularity,
touched by radiation that bears your name.
The dreamlike, disembodied voice resounds
through silence, stripped of all those accidents
of man; intimate as any machine:
impersonality that breaks the heart;
the congregation's ears penetrated
by strange words that echo through galaxies.

Your expressive eyebrows ascend and fall
as you slyly wink at the Creator
whose cunning mind you expect soon to know.
You intersperse your universal sermon
with witticisms, anxious to reveal
that, like Him, you're no stranger to a joke:
authors both of little-read bestsellers,
questions with answers no one can translate;
immune to time but not to suffering,
lost among those interstellar spaces.

Like disintegrating comets, your eyes
burn, fixed beneath footlights that soon will fade
into that curved past where the future resides,
leaving your transatlantic voice behind:
that advertiser's dream that will live on
without the body it never possessed,
persuading us to go on conversing,
whatever the cost, as those radio
telescopes lengthen into the night sky
to catch echoes of voices not our own.

From the *Tractatus** to *Teletubbieland*

*According to her husband, Iris Murdoch, in the grip of Alzheimer's
disease, derived rare moments of comfort from watching* Teletubbies.

Only in moments does consciousness grow clear
like a brief flame risen from moistened peat
and, with the self's emergence, comes the fear
of the return to that black winding-sheet
that binds and smothers the once lucid mind
that penetrated the propositions
of the *Tractatus*. Like Ivan in his sack,
you struggle to break loose but cannot find
the opening to daylight's dimensions.
You reverse through darkness, driven far back

to bathe in those flowered fields, stems rigid,
beneath the bright sun's laughing, baby face
stuck in a high, arching sky of vivid,
bounded blue, before Copernicus.
There you roam through long days with potbellied
children who leap free of gravity's force
and fly kites that caress the firmament;
who live in a shadowless cave and eat jellied
custard that seeks out bowls; who sleep in peace,
safe where the mind's 'death is not an event

in life* in that republic where unlived poems
are banned in those inarticulate
symposiums of summer when love's clean halves join
and the windmill on the hill rotates
through stillness, lightening air like fire,
and rabbits graze beyond the reach of guns.
You shelter within those familiar stranger's hands
that cradle your unspeakable terror
as those round figures decline with the sun
into the silence that vibrates when music ends.

* *from* Tractatus Logico-Philosophicus *by Ludwig Wittgenstein*

Judith Lal

Upgrade

The day I left she held the small bird
of her heart against my ear.

There are thrushes here and I am blessed
by this I know, but it is nice to hear it said,
a mantra for days burnt out with poetry.

My mother says it on one of her visits
and it is nearly as nice as hearing the birds
themselves as they wobble with song.

On the new league of things it is not
about economy-class syndrome, social
evolution, conspiracy theory or sex and race,

it is how many rare bird types choose to dapple
the walls of the workplace. It has been writ before
how governments could fall or a sweatshop

might open in El Salvador, but I am happy
enough here for the moment tell her,

and today, asleep in their aviaries of stratosphere,
the swifts arrived in from Africa.

Getting On
for Lizzy

My friend and I have reached a certain point,
nights spent leafing through rabbit insurance policies.
The dwarf lop is part of the family

which makes me an aunty of sorts to
a hypoallergenic, plush bumbag,

or of the furnishings, as it burns doughnut-rings into the carpet,
trying to catch up with its own rabbit-self
or nudges a smell past the newel of the staircase.

It is a marshmallow deposit from the big bang and
how much of a rabbit it is depends on where you sit.

We sit tight and watch bunny try to see off
an inner ear infection as he slowly moves his head
from side to side sadly disagreeing with the world,

a blind man playing pianoforte
trying to shake out a seed of thought.

Seahorse and Climbing

Just moments before sugar rushes to an estuary of blood,
endorphins are on the swim and with a Lippizaner's head
on older shoulders, I stand too sharply from being bent
over a desk writing all morning. The doctor assures of low
pressure, a sign of good health in these times of abundant salt,

but for this vertigo the blame must lie with seahorses,
the way they rise in coupling and embrace
like tiny dragons, without the awkwardness of arms;
after a solitary existence hooked to seagrass,
crocheting the ocean beds of the South Pacific.

You shoot out from hip, our children that cause
no anxiety, pampered in their smallness.
These aquarium nights, we watch over them
as they skate between the teeth of white shark.

Chocolate Angel

You sometimes get to hear of their deeds
that range from the mundane to the miraculous,
helping with groceries or just sitting light as a
bag of sugar on the end of beds, and sometimes
we wish them a little more avenging, a little less sweet.

My grandfather was lucky enough to sight one
with my late grandmother's smile,
in a church in Jerusalem,

and only the other day, on the way back from booking
in an essay on 'Postcolonial Writing and the Migrant Eye',
one sat next to me at the bus stop. Her rose-carob wings
started to melt, on to the pavement, which didn't go
unnoticed by the man to the right of her:

you see that's what they do,
fucking wogs dirty the place up,
I'd send them all back tomorrow.

Katie Landon

It Was a Surrender, Not a Battle

I kept my eyes closed. I never glimpsed his face.
Lips and palms scrutinized what I could not gaze
upon. Shirking from my shock of snakes, the mane
Minerva melded – hexed my head – writhing bane
of a biography, penalty for pride –
I kept my eyes closed.

His whispers mixed with a susurrus hiss. Sweet
nothings are just that: nothing. Garden replete –
gorged with marble men, their skin glistens, rain clings
to them as women once did. He murmured things –
sword hummed. Sluiced air. Trophy head severed. Glare died.
I kept my eyes closed.

Sodom Burning

Did we run? I
can't remember now.
I recollect the sun's assiduous glare – sand slid
under foot, drifting, like ash – our home
burning. The wicked, now timber, set alight, a bonfire blazing behind
us, pulsing against our backs, licking

our heels. Sky
swallowed red. 'Now!'
she shrieked, voice crackling like kindling. 'Move quickly!' She slid
the curtain, shut the door to our home
for ever left behind
a daughter, listened for the scream, felt her ghost kicking

in her womb, slid
to a standstill, heat wavering, dipping into the folds of her skirt.
                                                                And now,
all I can see is her neck, twisting towards home,
craning to find

how far the flames had feasted – slid
their fiery fingers around what is now
a desert, a ghost, my mother – a stone,

a landmark families casually slide
their hands down, how

they smooth their fingers against her skin as I once did.

Vacation

This: it is not quite what she had in mind.

Struggling behind him,
suitcase lurching on an uneven walkway –
stones shift and scatter,
her ankle longs to twist painfully,
it wants to make her fall.

In a fantasy akin to a wedding cake ornament
she envisioned herself, arm linked with his,
sipping from a fluted glass of inexpensive champagne
(for even in her dreams he remains frugal).

Instead, he drank Coors from a can
and flipped through all 217 channels.
Later, he passed out,
can in hand,
on top of the scratchy motel bedspread.

Staring at the ceiling,
limbs dragging under the weight of his snores,
she noticed a water stain in the shape of a horse,
imagined nuzzling her face against its plaster mane,
feeding it an apple from a well-worn burlap sock.

She has become too old for this.

When the Phone Rings at 4 a.m., all I Hear Is Breathing

The spare bedroom no longer
lives up to its name.
Just leave, I say,
under my breath,
on the bottom step,
arms curved around
a laundry basket
brimming
with our dirty clothes.

The mirror tells me things
I tell myself
to disregard, but the words itch –
gather expectant on my lips
like the pressure of a first kiss.

Reactions[2]

We eat our dinner silently.
Your fork scrapes the plate,
metal on bone,
accentuates
the quiet
carved out
around us.

Knuckles white,
I fix my fist,
clench the butter knife tight.
Its blade:
serrated,
too dull.
Immune to nothing
I fold
and sweep
and wash
and wait.
Create a space
safe enough to hide in.

I can smell her hair
on your hands.
She breathes between us –
pulsates
behind your closed eyes,
white, like light.

Your keys hang on a nail by the door.
I watch them fall from your pocket
to the hardwood floor
of her foyer,
tugging at your belt,
pulling off her blouse.

I unearth a moment of us
in the past.
Happy.
I suspend it above me,
just out of reach,
and spend the afternoon
standing on a metal stool
in the kitchen
attempting
to touch it.

Sarah Law

Twelve-Foot Lizards

People do go through life believing all sorts of things
and don't necessarily get themselves sectioned
although the most persuasive of them perhaps should
seeing that they can cause distress to others

such as David Icke who had that famous breakdown
and then appeared on Wogan wearing turquoise
and declared himself to be the son of God
and was completely discredited in the public eye

you would have thought he'd become such a headcase
that he'd soon be back under medical supervision
although he's managed to write books and even tour
and his wife and himself do all this publishing

but this thing about the lizards, why it's ridiculous
he must have watched that children's sci-fi programme
years ago about an alien race taking over
as that's more or less his thesis

twelve-foot lizards ruling the world, including
royalty, politics and the light entertainment industry
morphing themselves in and out of human shape
and killing with a flick of the tongue

and he comes out with all this in a kind of naïve
innocence, resisting all accusations of racism
although he tries to tone it down at public seminars
but people love to goad him on

as if there's a subterranean kind of sympathy
those dreams you had when young and never quite
got rid of; all the neighbours turning into beasts
and skeletons inhabiting the lounge at night

so that it was sometimes possible to believe these things
in an almost reassuring way, and that at other times
they would herald terror like a cold rod
against which there was only singing and a foetal curl

and finally a screaming which would bring help
and light and a hand on your brow
and relief, sweet, like some kind of reward

The Man with a Passion for Pots

From music he was moved
to aesthetics of earthenware,
roundly falling in love with the mould
and the curve of the craft. He could see
them everywhere, each whispering
rich with their own harmonics,
hungry for him to take them up,
curate them, reflower them,
and make with them a life.

From amateur he moved
to heady expertise, spanning
the delicate porcelain,
the rowdy toby jugs. He
thought it a laugh when presented
with one in his own image.

His face was growing rough by then
and set with his own success.
And each day brought him a fresh one,
as, guru-wise, he sent the punters
into an antique flutter. He loved the girls
who brought to him their undiscovered beauty.
Often he saw them home in a taxi,
lured them onto his show.

In later years he simplified his tastes
and laid aside the gaudy and the great,
from Chinese Dynasty and Clarice Cliff,
he settled down to muted browns and creams.

He took delight in pouring out his tea
and watching as the light ribboned its stream,
the warm weight shifting from pot to cup,
and each set in its place, in ordered leisure.

He thought about his life
eccentric beyond measure
and laughed aloud –
an empty vessel
filling him with pleasure.

Nigel Lawrence

Found Poem

It was just where I thought it would be,
a little out of sight,
like grit in the corner of my eye.
I had to pretend I'd not seen it,
or felt its breath on my cheek,
or its subtle scent,
sharp as lime juice on the tongue.

I was prepared for the waiting game.
Adjusted my clothes,
undid another button,
put on my sunglasses,
acted like I'd never been here before.
I walked on,
with the eyes in the back of my skull
mapping its progress like a blip on a radar.

Until
the screen blanks me.
Casual as a duck on a boating lake
I turn around. Unbalanced, senseless,
heart bouncing like a telegraph wire,
waiting for the sudden crack
of words escaping through bone.
Last thing I remember
a flash of blood through the eyes,
smell of piss
hot as hopelessness.

Identification

You come around,
find the car is leaving Turin
for the mountains.
The sun bursts on and off
through the mountain tunnels.
The consul is taking his time.
His small talk drowns
in the gush of the air conditioner.
You hear her voice in your head
tell you not to do it. Hear your own
in reply: *but what choice do I have?*
Kiss me. Goodbye. First, the police station
where an officer empties a wet plastic bag:
keys, crampons, paraphernalia.
You have been imagining
tiled benches,
white sheets pulled back,
eyes meeting, nods, then
a shaking cigarette in a corridor
that smells of vomit.
But here is an unclinical box of a room
and the smell of nothing.

Someone places a footstool in front of you
on flagstones uneven as rumours.
You stay standing, but later remember
and realize they thought you'd need it.
Shake your head, try to clear it
of the ache of travel and thin air.
Watch as the police officer
opens a cabinet in the wall
and slides a body out
dressed for February
though it is now late August
and hot as a beach outside.
You remember what you've been told
about the ice, but still wonder
why someone has melted the face,
reset the nose and lips
in the wrong places, wonder
why it is still wearing gloves,
then realize it isn't.
You say what you came here to say
and hear it taken away by other lips,
translated, written down, brought back
to sign, countersign, sign.
You are now driven
to a hotel by a river. On the way
the consul congratulates you
and you half expect to find
a certificate of competence
among the wallet of papers on your lap.
Instead you find a hole in your chest,
flashbacks, the impotence of alcohol,
ten years with no remission.
You hear her tell you again.
Still feel the echo of the same reply.

The Pathologists Play Pass the Parcel

We sit in our usual circle
but today hands come after feet.
I get passed one big as a shovel
with nails like fountain-pen nibs.
The lifeline is woeful.

The music starts again.
It is time to pass.
Then follow: kidney, liver, lung, spleen,
a dick limp as a dead bird.
In the silence I catalogue them,
their defining features: scar tissue, warts,
unusual associations of pale yellow fat,
but don't feel able to put a name to them.

The game is over.
We put our smiles back on,
use our own eyes
to find cars
parked out in the dark.

John McCullough

Bridal Shower

It began in the bedroom:
soft sprinkle on sheets
then onto the floor – insidious, snaking
under the door, licking over the varnish
of freshly sheened stairs.

Water now fills the kitchen –
they can't speak for the snorkels,
can't hear for their own
tireless babble of gas;
every meal is made through

the plumb slowness of ocean,
badly stomached amid bilious
gulpfuls of sluice,
their one expression
the faceless gaze of the frogman.

She swims out to her coral-pink
reef of azaleas, a sunlounger, dank paper.
Sky infuses her lungs. She'd like to climb
over the fence to next door
but keeps tripping on flippers.

Him? He is shameless,
takes to the pub in his wetsuit,
elsewhere after that.
Always back by morning
to fish for the post;

their eyes catch in the hallway,
fixate on the bubbles
streaming up from the other
which mean nothing, nothing but air.

That Marjorie

She finds herself blonde and frail
in the mirror: tongueless, pale as old bread,
her butter hair thinly spread, brittle with bleach.
She's only teasing the scissors

when, snip-hungry, they snap
and commence war without warning,
the fall of the first lock
attended with a gasp.

With each chop, her blue eyes
become freer, harder:
no flinch with the final
close of the blades.

She slicks it through with conditioner,
scrunches as she rinses,
so pleased with the feel
of new moss on her skull.

Now she is all rock, *that* woman again:
the human salamander they threw into the sun
who came back with a tan
and glistening with steam.

'Welcome back Marjorie.'

Next time they watch her
peg up the week's sheets,
they'll see an angry head
round and brown as a stoat's.

Firm as toast,
she'll prune down the apple tree,
buy a wardrobe of suede.
Noisily, she'll teach herself DIY.

The long strands wait in a bag till midnight
when there's just enough breeze.
Leant out of her bedroom window with a fistful,
she lets the wind take it,

watches it blown out over the roofs,
tinged with moonlight,
falling like tickertape
on all the parked cars.

Christine McNeill

The Ringing of Words

They came like balloons:
Live piano music! Dance!

How words laugh at us
for no reason.

How you can weep in them
without me knowing.

And what we see –
a dancefloor, fingers stroking

keys, and our steps
turning in on themselves

somewhere in the words;
your arms feeling available space

for the body you love –
I breathe in everything the words evoke –

breathe it like fragrance coming from nowhere:
what we never had but think we had,

or believe was owed to us.
Dance, you said –

in that word I ate a whole cake.
And: *Then I can hold you in my arms.*

Then. Then. In all the sounds
I failed to recognize it.

But *'then'* stayed awake. Listen
how it now brings relief.

Yes – *then.*
Look how swiftly it moves us on.

Driven

A lonely road up into French hills.
It is dusk. He drives so fast,
keeping his foot down even on
bends, mocking that sudden
spark of fear – but really the fear is singing,
and he marvels at how smooth the wheels
grip – like gliding over the shell of an egg.

What lies beyond the windscreen
borders on God: trees without beginning
or end. *Give me a dog, or a house,*
flits through his mind, and then her way
of cracking an egg or topping a soft-boiled one.
The vision of her quietly looking
frees and entraps him.

Speed. Danger. Being in control,
being his own man, his own master –
rigid and mute;
her taking the first spoonful of warm yolk –
the moment when something in him
starts to confess: watch how soon
it turns into a lie that steers him home.

Break-in

Frantic calls –
the lawn dive-bombed where the neighbour's cat
slunk away without prey –
but the damage was done: the nest ripped,
the young either clawed or dead from fright.
For nearly an hour the blackbirds freewheeled:
bringing food to what had vanished.
The streetlights came on,
and still they perched on the hedge
looking for signs in the silence . . .

It was the way I found you
when answering your distressed *please come*:
by the slashed bed littered with drawer-contents.
The silence in the room a second monstrous break-in.
Only a small vase, copper-fumed, had been left
untouched: a purple rim from which
rainbow colours unravelled –
you'd bought it as an image of wholeness –
so light in my palm that I feared
it might break.
Once, watching a bird on the appletree,

we read *wonder* in its eyes
as its head tilted towards the sun;
curiosity at a movement on a branch below;
fear at the swooping of wings overhead –
a second's blissful calm before all this
repeated itself, quicker, twice over,
and when we marvelled at the bird's ability
to bear so much experience in so short a time,
it made off through the sun-burnished branches . . .

I remembered all this
as I handed you the vase,
and you trembled.

Mating Call

He tries so hard –
almost topples off the fence,
losing the string of plummy sounds.

She, attempting to unhook his
love interest, flutters up and
down, shaking a bag of obscure selves.

He whistles from a thrilled belly –
a needlepoint ambush
that has her fleeing into the guttering.

How deft they play:
she, cowering under the rosebush;
he, luring air to be on his side.

And I think of you, eyes closed in the grass –
with so much sun in your smile
that it makes me fall upwards.

Julius Man

the house is a jigsaw unfinished

the house is a jigsaw unfinished
broken side wall with bricks missing kids' toys abandoned
at the upvc front door a satellite dish slanted skewered
sludge-coloured sill paint peels like dry skin

on the driveway a guy works clangs with fat fingers of tools
operating on the metal gut of his mud-splattered truck he doesn't
notice underneath the leaked glum-glop of oil the syrupy black
and that stuck in the black-hole gum a swallowtail flaps
with berserk desperation ariel-pronged antennae try to sense sense
and there it is again

how his body must've swung from the climbing frame
on some freezing awful morning lifeless as a pupae
hung limp amid the skeletons of swings slide and
quiet playthings planted into the asphalt of the park

maybe he hoped that like fast-eating caterpillars
he too would be bigger brighter and that the uniform world
would be drenched in the syrupy glow of a sun-drenched
weekend no skool no timetables but perfected in amber

cows just meander off

cows just meander off in an unhurried waddle
their pink udders swinging like movie cowboys
with low-slung holsters cracking one or two jokes with a moo –
and they march against the barbed wire fence
that is two ribbons on either side of the path people walk on –
which slips down into other fields, a snaky lane, a distance –

grass tufts poke slyly through – the cows look enviously
then turn away – probably cross-bred amnesia

Jill Maughan

How Are You?

'How are you?' you ask lightly.
'Okay, okay,' I reply,
but I lie.

Monday I cried for Paula Yates,
dead at forty.

Tuesday I felt for me,
stumped by loss at forty-two.

Wednesday got drunk,
wished for you.

Thursday rained.

Friday swept by.

Saturday was blue.

Sunday cut.

There, there, does that answer you?

Dear Love

We cannot go to the sea,
for the sea is not the same any more.

We cannot drive northward
looking at houses, for the houses
don't trust our speculation.

And southward to the woods
is out, we cannot go southward to the woods
because the woods don't like us.

I cannot sit in your flat,
your flat has been unkind to me.

You cannot sit in my house,
my house is too nervous to be sat in.

We cannot go east to the hills,
I asked them and the hills
said not to come.

We cannot ride westward to the moors,
for the granite-tough moors
always speak their mind.

We cannot go back,
back is too littered with sad remains.

We cannot go forward,
forward will not even offer us
a one-night board . . .

Love, you must meet me now
on some other plane,
in the slippery shadows of dreams,

down an avenue not yet made,
by a tree not planted, under a sky
we never could have imagined.

Burn

It flares in the dark,
shiny as flame,
so we call in for their stopwatch

fast, sizzling hot,
fried Big Macs.
You at sixteen

love making things burn,
love the racing red
fire engines that run

to your hoax calls.
With one simple strike
you torch what others create,

and watch, with pounding heart,
the firemen gyrate
to your loony tune.

You're very dangerous, Caroline.
I think it as we sit opposite
and you grin and chew,

and the warm, blood ketchup
dribbles on your chin.
Your reasons? There are a few –

Mam's an alcoholic,
Dad's a violent bastard . . .
You hate them both,

but him, him the worst,
he chokes your throat.
That evening, after I drop

you back at the home,
what memories ran
through your head,

as you locked the door,
lit the curtains,
sat back on the bed?

Cold as blue ice,
prepared to melt,
did you plan to rise again,

heralded by the wail
of the fire engines, virgin and new,
a phoenix-like, spectral wisp called *you?*

Andrew Mayne

Kal Iblur's Trajectory

I ask you to imagine what it took to wait, packed in there,
primed for the big bang – having done it a hundred times . . .

Course, I got sick of all those smart alecky jossers always
bursting to tell me how we worked it: now you thought

you saw me loaded, but it was really my double stowed
away in the cannon's pedestal; then, under the cover-daze

of that shuddering bang and lashings of smoke, money
for old rope to whip off the sheet from the big top's side

(hard to miss that cue, but it happened). Leaving everyone
gawp-and-gasping at the charcoal-edged star-shaped rent . . .

Until . . . enter me! Dancing, waving down the aisle, all tatty
and chimney-sooted, with dabs of self-raising on my hair.

In fact, I worked it from both ends – turn and turn about.
Never claimed to be the bloody Zacchinis. Franklin's

always was a small-time show for towns out in the sticks.
Still, you saw the country from end to end. Time and time

again – in fact, for forty years. Spent mostly on the point
of extinction. Pitching the big top by some rubbish tip or

sewage works; fuzzy with a hangover in a muddy field;
most days, two two-hour shows. Always moving on;

usually treated like scum. Of course, I'm past it now,
the life of the road, as past it as the smell of naphtha.

*

Started as a tumbler with some clowning thrown in. Always
taken for granted – two or three general dogsbodying jobs.

Worked the wall of death for a time – glad to be relieved
from swilling out the cages when I was twenty-three.

In tights, then, as light on my feet on the trampoline as any
Claude Copper ballet prancer – though first scene played as

the berk, an L plate on my back, outsize bowler, braces
hoisting up and down a *Come Dancing* suit ten times too big.

But soon to be the stooge who suddenly takes wings.
There was the dog act. Poncy black and white yapping poodles.

Then the big gun until bad health finally caught up with me.
Now my hearing's completely shot, I find I'm writing much more.

Been told the story of my life could be worth something.
Though stuff about circuses is said to be old hat. Behind

my time again! Yet, who knows? I'm still aiming for an even style.
But I've got down its last sentence finale already – courtesy

of Herbert Franklin, owner and ringmaster for fifty years,
who could do the build-up spiel like no one else. When I

finally packed it in, he said – handing me the envelope with
the forty quid in it, all in fat white fivers – 'Discharge papers,

Kal. You'll be a bugger to replace.' Then, his expression
going all serious – I'd started to expect something just like

a face full of confetti from the old red fire bucket – he said:
'Kal, these days it's hard to find men of your . . . quality.'

Open Evenings

'Welcome to the English Building . . .'

(Welcome for the two hundredth and sixty-sixth time.)
'I have a leaflet here that I would like you to take –
it lists our aims and aspirations . . .' The spiel that follows
comes in several variations – mainly designed to keep
me (in my smartest, most uncomfortable suit) sane.

This circuit, one stern young couple ask: 'What will you do
to get our son reading?' I affirm that I will share my own
enthusiasms, take him regularly to our Junior Library with
its special stock of books; there'll be a new 'class reader'
every four weeks or so, creative writing will spin off . . .

'We have been informed,' they say, 'that the key to his whole
educational future depends on him becoming a regular reader.'
They make reading sound like some exceptionally unlikely activity –
like training junior astronauts for flights to Mars. 'Pupils are
encouraged to keep reading logs; the School runs a bookshop . . .'

And so on . . . The Burs' look of being very unimpressed deepens –
unless I misread their stony glare. It's the quick fix they're after
I guess, and ask: 'Do you do much reading, then, yourselves?'
Should I prevent them moving somewhat sorrowfully on their way?
Instead, I feel just now in need of a good shot of print myself –

something spontaneous and spare. Hors de combat, I'm drawn to
a retreat upstairs; down the long unlit corridor, quite off circuit
on tonight's grand tour, I'll pull the Book Store's dark eiderdown
over me – its smells of damp pakamacs and mouldy biscuits –
and light up page after page with a pocket torch. Night after night –

did I ever say thank you for all those bedtime stories? Probably
Mother guessed, quite early on, I arranged my own extra rations.
I'm tracking that couple along the downstairs corridor as they head,
boy-guided and broodily muttering, towards the New Computer
Block.
'Here, do please let me give you a reading list before you go.'

Why Is It

some poems seem to end as finished as the loose
        nowness
of a shirt or jacket thrown over the back of a chair,
        but then start
to look bedraggled – so you reach for the jangling hangers
        in the wardrobe;
while others you spend hours refolding, tucking them
        carefully away –
a jigsaw of tight repositionings in the compact suitcase –
        only to end up,
when you reach your holiday destination, scattering them
        with relief
all over the spare bed where they look
        so accessibly just right?

Jenny Morris

Cul-de-Sac

At the first house lives
a man who laughs in his sleep.
His ugly wife is jealous
of his secret life. She wants
to take a hatchet to him.

At the next house is a girl
who wears dark glasses, shroud clothes.
'She never gets a single Christmas
card,' says the knocking postman.
She doesn't give a kiss for his bills.

At number three is the youth
who collects glass eyes.
He lines them up on windowsills
looking out. They shudder
when he plays Wagner full blast.

See, hear and speak no evil
on Death Row, thinks the postman.
No one's ever home for those
packets and big envelopes
at the bottom of his lonely bag.

Risky Ticking at the Core

Footless bird flutters.
This heart hops in its cage
with unsteady hammer blows.
Dancing time is past.
Keystone no longer stout.
Blood torrents slow
to a seepage
through dark red valves.
Gnarled old ball of secrets
tries to repeat its refrain,
stumbles and shakes,
a tumbler sensing danger.
Stunts and twists pull bones
in their bleak rooms.
It's a guide, a knotted fist
punching a way out
of the broken home.

Altar to the Unknown God

This is for you. Written words left out.
Oak leaves caught the early light,
watched you, green eyes in trees
on those North York moors.
Your time drained away until insects
nested in your hair and those
foreign leaves rose from your eyes
under the earth.

On this side of darkness
empty wings beat in the woods
by the brick ponds. Your dream head,
a paper lantern glowing in my night.

Your boy's life glimpsed through photographs,
sfumato, cocooned in your father's
summerhouse as an amber fly.
Round eyes over your infant's mug
of goat's milk. Your cloth doll swung by its feet.
Round glasses hiding that sad look,
a shyness. Sent away young to the choir school
in Low Skellgate. Such neat hair,
shining smile, a preciseness.
You held up the pumpkin as an offering.

I hold your afternoon photos of Karachi,
note your interest in bazaars, mosques,
palaces, camel carts, water wheels, beggars,
scribes, knife grinders, a small man
skinning a kid.

Kindness follows you around.
Your books, annotated in tiny script,
line my walls. That black silk gown
with silver daisies you gave your mother –
I wore it to shreds.

After the dregs of the day you learned
loneliness, secrecy and despair.
Did the leaves whisper warning signs?
You saw gaudy muslins, crumbling towers,
bursting fruit, flesh, a triangle of sky,
rain and tumbling stars. You heard
nightmare wings rustling and scented almonds.
You chose to die without explanation
and slipped away, silent in Delhi,
city of the shadowless djinns.

James Oliver

What I've Been Doing

'Do you know what you've been doing?
You've been staring at that sign
For over an hour. We've watched you.
We've been sitting in the patrol car watching you.'

'You've been staring at that sign.'
'There's something I'm trying to remember.'
'We've been sitting in the patrol car watching you.'
'If I stare at this sign long enough maybe I'll know what to do.

There's something I'm trying to remember.'
The sign is for Great Yarmouth and Ipswich.
'We've been sitting in the patrol car watching you.
Do you need any help?'

The sign is for Great Yarmouth and Ipswich.
'We've watched you for over an hour.
Do you need any help?
Do you know what you've been doing?'

On looking at a picture of
a reclining bodhisattva figure . . .

Look up through the glass bricks
In the roof of the hallway
Outside the nurses' station of the
Male ward of the psychiatric hospital.

Look up, and stand there not moving
Staring at the light coming from the day outside.
What are you trying to see?
What are you trying to remember?

Look up. Why do you look up?
It's natural to look down when you are depressed.
You are not completely depressed though;
There is a part of you straining for the light, like a flower.

Look up. But don't look up at the ceiling.
That is to take the gesture of the bodhisattva figure
Too literally.

Helen Oswald

Listing

It only takes a glimpse of listings
or a billing on a board for me to feel
that clutch of panic in the gut. The sense
that you are somewhere seeing something
I am not.
That some painting or play
is making your heart beat
faster. That you are turning
your head to someone, to smile
or nod at some wry remark.
Or you are
at a concert with your eyes shut,
a cello's slow bowing vibrating
in the dark caves of your chest.

This is all I feel now, so long
after it was me you turned to
in the night when the concert hall was quiet
and miles away and I was close. In sleep
your hand would settle on me like a butterfly –
I dared not breathe or move for fear
it would fly off.

It only takes a listing or a billing now
for me to feel
I am missing something.

Letter From Above Ground

Here I am, facing the year you could
or would not face – your thirty-fifth.
Half your bible allotment.
It looks like this:

in the distance the Downs are turning green,
trees feather their nests,
balance a trapeze of skinny births.
Some will fall without a safety net.

Seagulls show their white crowns to the sky,
dapple the roofs with shit.
There is a gravity that pulls all things
both to the earth and under it.

And yet the planet hurtles through on quiet engines.
Today is Sunday. The kettle cools its breath.
I wash my hair, dead already they tell me,
and note the slippery virulence of death.

Late trains sashay right and left across the viaduct,
brash chorus lines, batting their eyes at the sun.
The arches long to cool their thighs,
in the brown sea beyond. Their day will come.

On tennis courts the balls rock back and forth
swung in a cat's cradle of white lines.
We used to play but never kept the score.
Fifteen, thirty love. No more.

Birthday

On his 80th birthday your father dozed
between folds of a paper that told him
daily his world had spun away,
like a dancer swung out at a ball.

The music had changed and he no longer
knew the steps, or that there were none,
but he knew the dance hall and in his day
had been a chooser of red paint.

Now, retired soldier, teacher, preacher, he wears
tweed and dates himself with every word
he speaks – John the Baptist, Solzhenitsyn, Yeats,
gifts he unwrapped slowly for you all.

You dread his going, like Santa,
his sack still full of history and bad jokes,
of Ireland in the thirties, times that changed,
which, in his last days, was his one complaint.

Confirmation

He laid his broad, soft palms
on rows of well-combed heads
and gave us brand new, holy names.
He wore a hat and purple dress
I learned to call a 'mitre', 'cassock'.

New words were mysteries then
and never seemed to fit. A hassock
should have been a bale of hay;
a pulpit, a small, blue egg, one end
soft, like a baby's unknitted skull.

We called him Peter, a name
full of the Galilean importance
of fish, sliding and glinting like coins,
and deftly mended nets I visualized
as mum's miraculous string bag.

There was magic everywhere.
I used to press my ear against
the chest of day, listening
for breaths drawn in the shadows,
ghosts in the cold morning air.

Assurance

Dear Sir,
I see that what I am is worth
less than the sum of all my parts,
that's twenty thousand pounds to be precise,
upon my accidental death, or rebirth.

Whereas, I understand that total loss
of two fine limbs is £30,000;
an elbow £7,000; a hip or thumb six grand,
though for my little toe you do not give a toss.

There are some parts which you omit to mention
and which I'd badly miss if they were gone,
or if from overuse they ceased to function.
I hope a hefty sum is your intention.

I see I am not covered if my lover
breaks my heart or if I get blind drunk,
cut off my nose to spite my face, get tongue-tied,
put my foot in it and don't recover.

The same applies if I should peg out
footloose high up on some Himalayan peak,
riding the Tour de France, or fighting
at a football match with Krauts.

But on the other hand (that's fifteen thousand),
if I sit safely at my desk all day
then fall under the number 38 on my way home
to watch TV, everything will be just grand.
Sir,
I would like to sign up to your policy
but one thing bothers me –
where do I collect the dosh when I am gone,
and what the fuck do you propose I spend it on?

Dean Parkin

Buggerlugs

School was a joke for you, Bugsy,
like inking the four corners
of Stephen Hamble's rubber
and waiting for the blue
to invade his map of Europe.
I laughed, but later
you were less appreciated,
when the rest of the kids grew
serious, started working,
revising for 'O's and 'A's.
Some teacher you were lippy to
barked back, 'If you want to be
a petrol pump attendant all your life
you're going the right way about it.'
But you knew of a job laying pipes
in Jo'berg, where the real dosh was;
could afford to scoff at Paul
sending off to the GPO
and Eggy at the leccie company
like his dad. Last time we spoke
you were *Outta here*, on your bike
with the handlebars turned
the wrong way. You passed
the school bus and I watched you,
not stopping for the red light,
up the pavement and cutting through

the Shell garage, then
back on the road again,
freewheeling, no hands.

Hot Dog

The smell of hot dogs reminds him
of how he used to like them, how long it's been
since he had one and with plenty of time,
five minutes to kill and five minutes
to get to the interview five minutes early,
he joins the queue. Orders a jumbo, agrees
to onions, foolishly adds brown sauce
which slips off the sausage and gathers
into a slick which starts to drip out of the roll,
dribbles over his cuff, cries on his tie, runs
down his shirt. The streaks on his chin
he smears with a tissue, spreads to his cheek,
even manages to rub some on his forehead,
and with time escaping, as the last slither of onion
skids down his jacket, he has to run.
It's further than he thought but, arriving late,
still has to wait, the secretary telling him to sit
and stay, offering him a chair in the exact spot
where the sun cuts across the room. Left alone,
panting, pulling at his collar, gently frying in the heat,
he realizes he smells of onions, finds his fingers
tainted with grease, just as the boss appears
and wants to shake him by the hand.

The Big Five-O

Happy Birthday! Tom – 50. The crude lettering,
okay, the five is bigger than the zero but the fifty
is the most noticeable thing, painted on a sheet,
tied to a fence by a roundabout. Let's hope it raises
the smile intended as Tom hurries to the office.

Something to kick him out of step, to remind him
that someone cares, this is how he should take it,
driving back home that night for a surprise party,
his wife at his elbow, teenage kids tamed at his feet,
while friends propose a toast and raise their glasses.

And the next day as he slows at the roundabout,
the banner is still there and perhaps even his smile
but it's there the next day and the next and each morning
spelt out in foot-high letters with balloons attached,
Tom has to be told he's fifty, like he can't remember.

And the next day it rains and the letters start to run
as the wind beats the sheet and a corner rips
until it droops on the fence with the shrivelling balloons,
the wishes now a wet blanket slapping the pavement.
He should take the damn thing down himself but can't

imagine wrestling with the soggy sheet or picking
a fight with knots, so instead he avoids the roundabout,
takes another route which could almost be quicker,
if he breaks the speed limit along Elmtree Road, where
the policeman clocks him pushing fifty in a forty zone.

The Last Customer

This one has nowhere to be
or if he has it's somewhere alone,
so you're his last contact of the day
and he's not letting go easily.
There's a book he wants ordered
if he could remember the title
or author, is it Mantripp, Manthorpe
or Longthorn, it might come back to him
and if it did could we order it?
Yes, another day perhaps,
but he's not finished yet, tries again,
goes through his shopping, shows me
the price of jam, two for one,
a bag of tangerines, reduced to this.
He'll be on his way now, he expects
I'll want to close, asking me for the time
as he backs off, retreats to the pavement.
Locking the door between him and me,
I wave, wish him goodnight through the glass,
when actually it's only late afternoon
and the whole evening looms ahead.

Her White House

The house was no longer there for her
and now she had nowhere to go
when she was miserable.

The rooms were in the right order,
everything in its place, even the scissors
had a nail of their own.

Some of her elephants lived above the jars of pasta
in the kitchen, ebony black against the pink walls.
There were painted chairs with a plain pine table

and a staircase hidden in a cupboard. This led
to her favourite room, which had the evening sun
and a big blue armchair where she could nestle

and read the books shelved around the walls.
There was a desk and a table, big enough
for big books. And she could sew here,

make curtains for the whole house.
This was a room in which she could spread out
her patchwork and leave it undisturbed.

Downstairs was for visitors, a front
room suitably pastelled, cream and peach,
to deal with sudden company.

The bedroom was a room to wake up in.
She saw it as a Larsson print, adding Bear Peter
and a bed made with blankets and fresh sheets.

The bathroom was blue because it could be.
Facing south, it didn't need warm colours.
And the seat was never left up.

At the top of the house was a room undecorated,
full of things she didn't want today, a box of Lego,
the Brio railway, held in hope of any grandchild.

It was a white house, close to where she had to be,
the closest she could get to running away,
but she'd never been inside and now it was sold.

Simon Pettifar

Small Change

In anticipation, the Cabin Crew Director
Thanks us 'on behalf of the world's children'
For placing any change we have and do not need
In the 'Change for Good' envelope
Which each of us can find
In the seat pocket right in front of us.
Yes please, I'll have some of that, you bet!
The thanks of the world's children?!
Some of that, for just these coins?
Take them, take them quickly, right away!
I don't care how tiny a portion of that stuff I get
For . . . what is it, let's see, 2 marks 60 . . .
If it's only one smile, one glimpse of a smile,
One moment of light in an eye,
One small spark of the thanks of the world's children,
Then it's the best bargain I have ever known.
In fact, I think I'll give all that I own.

Shudder

You broke out of your cell.
No you didn't.
You were let out of your cell and ever since
have been so busy *gambolling*
you've only just seen
– from your fear of *real* freedom –
that you are, merely, outside the prison block
but well within the prison grounds.

Crack your life open.
No, not like a nut,
not like a little toothsome nut.
I don't mean break it like bread, like a honeycomb.
I mean:
Smash it open!
I mean:
Take up the sledgehammer!
I don't want to see anything but
specks of dust
on the wind.

Kristine in Denmark

On Sundays
Kristine in Denmark
goes to the forest
to scream.
Kristine takes the subway
out of the city,
leaves the cars and houses behind her,
enters the forest and
sets about it.
She picks her spot.

She opens her face to the sky.
She opens her mouth to the weak winter sun and
in it all comes and
out it all comes,
frightening the squirrels.

Think of Kristine, if you like,
on Sundays.
Think of her, if it helps.
There she is, bellowing away
in the forests on the edge of Denmark.
She is Sexton's purple crocus
blowing its way out of the snow.
She is blowing her way out of the blizzard of past.
She is getting her work done.

Noble Silence Meets the Male Ego

We are enjoined to keep for nine days
Noble Silence
– silence of mind, silence of body, silence of speech.

No writing materials.
No reading materials.
No music.

No speech, no gesture, no eye contact.

Needless to say, the sexes have been segregated.

From the men's side of the hall, in meditation,
a constant battery of breaking wind, coughs and raucous sneezes,
shuffling, yawning, sudden scratchings, burps, hiccups.
Or, in other words:
'I'm still here!' 'Look at me!' 'Don't forget about me!'
From the women, nothing.

Only, now and then, a little sneeze.
Every two or three days, say.

The Cartwheel

Weren't you the one who did the cartwheel on Day Three?
That subtle surreptitious flick you gave your head
to ascertain there was no one around,
which yet missed me, just behind you on the path,
the way your arms flew up into the sky,
that sudden little sideways hop and then
your lovely roll onto your palms and on your feet again,
and me exhilarated, while you, hands in pockets, hunched again,
                                                    walked on,
as if I'd seen a sudden-bursting bud or star.

But surely it was you? – I noted the pattern of your jacket,
how your head looked from behind and
I've looked forward to this day and meeting you.

You laugh, enjoy the image too,
but no, you say, it was not you,
then jokingly you ask around.
Faces brighten at the thought,
all look at me amused but
no, you say, all of you say,
it was not you, it was not
you.

Lynne Rees

Cold

She likes the cold,
steps out of the house each morning
to feel the frost. When he calls her in
her hands are blue bones
translucent as skimmed milk.

At night she dreams of snow,
hers the only footsteps
puncturing the skin. She shivers
when they touch, when his breath, warm
breath trickles over her back.

The Woman in the Gutter

The woman in the gutter dressed very nicely
for someone in her position.

She didn't seem to mind if people
stopped and stared, or stepped over her.

Passing cars blew up leaves
and she brushed them away.

She even had patience with chewing gum.
A dog shat on her once and she

reapplied her lipstick, waited
three days for it to rain.

Once, when I was waiting to cross,
I felt a finger brush the curve of my heel.

But I may have been wrong.

Moving Pictures

From the dark of the yard
the bright kitchen window's my movie screen,
each grand gesture performed within a frame.

Arm curved, she pulls back
hair from her face, eyes wide
in the silence. He lifts his hands,
hits the table – an inaudible slap –
cheeks plump like apples,
mouth caverning with something
that could be laughter.
Her lips open. 'Stop' or is it 'Help!'
on a flickering caption,
the heroine tied to the rails,
the hero fighting with a moustachioed man,
the threat of steam at the bend in the track.

They both stop. Peer out into the darkness.
I raise my arms, bare my teeth
and rush at the window.

Jacqui Rowe

Weight Loss

Losing is one way:
      finding yourself without a father
on an early dark October night
     keeps you in size twelve
            or less,
  as he turns to ash as you turn to air
 giving someone back
     the space you take.
Discharging is another:
      they ask you how
         you keep so slim
     without the count except in bucketfuls
    of what comes out, calling it not
            an illness
   but the killing tightness of an eyebrow
  cured by acid cutting
      through your neck.
Wasting is the last:
     what invades and eats your guts
       tucks your stretchmarks from within,
 until all of you
    as elegant
    as hell
must learn to celebrate
    the triumph of the vacuum
         over nature.

Not Going

Reassurance that I
  do not
       climb through windows
          shadowless   seeking
    pavements tiled with
         microchips or ingots
what I own
except the cat
       hitched to a stick in a spotted cloth
  would not
        easing painfully across the sill
        stow away
my sea chest
    ending on the wild shore of Illyria
  am not
      Polly Oliver
        thigh slapping
           trailing
      after musketeers
    barely disguised
        as a girl
  will not
    my reclaimed music
         in a battered suitcase
        satin bound
          seek dining angels
      tuning northern   shoes
on gold
      bricked streets
  could not
     turn again
      to find the star and straight on
  to the pirates
    and the burning
      is that I am here.

Spaniel Bitch

The she-wolf draws
  her claws across my flagstones,
   waves her cubs by their neck scruffs,
  catching my look, baiting me
      to nurture and to fend.
  I nest in paper or beneath the table
    where his toe-caps miss
while her perfume seeps
   from the grass to the rug,
      dilating my eyes
   in the current of light and I am out
      in night-dressed forests,
  printing my pads on unspeaking leafpaths,
    knowing by what I breathe,
     keeping my own.
As I do not keep them now,
  walking to the pavement's rhythm,
    closer than
      a lead's length to his wrist.

Sibyl Ruth

Stepmother

I wasn't prepared for this.

The children in our room
at two, three a.m.
Their father's whispered *Ssh!*

Unsleeping hours
after every breach of the peace.

Lights to be left on in the hallway
just in case.

Dawn chorus of our washing machine.
Its relentless thump and swish.

Small pyjamas on our bathroom floor
like seaweed at low tide,
smelling urinous.

Whatever is given,
cola, milk, juice,
undergoes the same metamorphosis.

White flags of their sheets
at breakfast time
hanging over us.

Promise of one dry night
followed by nemesis.

Boy's scowling face.
The girl's distress.

My wish
to release a stream of words,
let them gush and hiss.

Needing to ease
a bursting bladder,
leak bitterness.

I'm talking enuresis.
Piss.

The Other

I could knock at your door on a weekday
and claim to be doing a survey.

There is information in your possession
which I'd find useful.

Already I know the code to your burglar alarm.
My spoon's gone in your dishes.

I stood at the door of your bedroom
eyeing your big silk jacket.

I was itching to try it on,
for the mirror to say who I'd become.

I found your low-fat spread inside the fridge,
your diet drinks in the cupboard.

I saw you on video:
a round-faced woman with the wrong haircut.

I picked up envelopes addressed to Mrs –
bank statements, car insurance.

I went swimming with your children,
seduced them with choc-ices, kindness.

This is the way we behave.
We could be an actress with two parts.

You leave. I arrive.
The neighbours must be laying bets.

They're taking sides.
We've got this much in common.

I know. You know.
I'm having your husband.

The Autobiography Class

He died you see,
says the lady. *My son.*
That's the reason I came.

There's a silk scarf tied at her throat.
She says, *We just stopped talking about him.*
It seemed a good way to cope.

A room put to different use, repainted.

It works, she says.
She is wearing a lambswool sweater
pinned with a gold brooch.

Half smiling, she says,
You start forgetting.
He began to disappear quite fast.

Black and white photos on a high shelf.

I may be remembering things wrong,
she says slowly.
Then shrugs inside her good coat.

Talk comes to a narrow place, backs away.

Her pale hair is beautifully set.
I want to write about him, she says,
but only the facts. Nothing creative.

Chairs spaced more widely round a table.

She says, *I buried him.*
I buried him inside me.

Robert Seatter

Paperweight

Now you are inside, with all those bits
of bright Murano glass. One to choose
among galaxy, garden, snow scene over Venice.
Now your eye like a marble, light on a curl
of your hair, the lip you have just licked,
harmony of your fingers and moons of your fingernails
are glass-cased, smooth to my touch.
I can look and look my fill inside – never catch you
blinking. I can never have enough of you.
Now I have you in the palm of my hand,
the warm and the cold of you.
Or here on the desk where you hold my life in place,
stop all my surfaces from sliding loose,
keep the best bits of me from blowing away.

The Dye-Maker

*Dye recipes were jealously guarded secrets. Sometimes they were even
bequeathed to the objects of unrequited love in the dye-maker's will.*
(Oriental Rugs: Antique & Modern)

Take cinnabar, indigo and alum –
you will have to climb hills, pull roots from rock
so you have the smell of it under your fingernails
and it will come back to you when you want it
least – turning a page, drawing a hand through
your hair. All the rooms full of it.
Grind and sift lighter than dust – these are the long hours
that will crack your fingers, coarsen your palms.
They will be hard for you who counted effort
as untruth, who having lost an instinct could never
have it back. There were even jokes you could never
laugh at a second time because the moment had gone.
Soak for ten hours, then drop the wool in and leave
to stain – this will be that feeling that invades you
so you cannot lift your head. The rooms will all be
one shape, one long, distant shade of purple.
And sometimes the days will be indecipherable too.
Mondays, Thursdays . . . you will not see them pass.
December will follow December.
Boil for three hours and wash in fresh water – still
there will be silence and the windows all steamed up.
You will write your name backwards on the glass,
but you will never see it right. You will stare and stare
at that vat of blue, the only blue you wanted.
Wash the wool again and beat in water – nothing
can rid you now of that spreading stain, its slow invasion.
Stare into the pool now you know its secret.
Observe how your fingertips have turned to blue.
One day every pore will breathe it.

Counting the Dots
After The Bridge at Courbevoie *by Seurat*

Days in this foreign city
when I forget my name, when I cannot order
even a coffee or a beer – my tongue a-tangle
with too many vowels, when I am invisible
to shop assistants, and the bus
does not stop for me.

Days when I disappear
into nothing, standing on this bank,
smelling the brown French clay, the snatch
and gone of autumn. From the bark against my hands
of the one black leafless tree, from the concrete groyne,
from the nudge and drag of boats at the quayside,

I shift into smoke, the issue from a steamer funnel
smudging the horizon, blurring the opposite bank,
the glitter of glasshouses that I know are there,
the clear procession of tomorrow which is Wednesday
towards Thursday, Friday –

a neat flotilla of boats in a line.
I count their invisible masts to make sense come,
count dot on dot on dot. All dots. Till I disappear.
Till I begin to count again.

Answerphone

I left you for a space calling out to me
like someone shouting across water
as if you knew for sure I was really there –

holding my breath below the surface,
pressure in my ears, cheeks like a football.
As if I might swim to the other side

with a change of clothes in a knotted plastic bag
and cycle off on a rusty bicycle
I had left behind the pine trees.

Then stand in some bar growing briefly light-headed
on a single glass of beer, walk out into sunshine
with no name, no home.

Oh sometimes I might think of you
as you followed me across the water,
as you spluttered and sank midway in the blue.

Knowing you, you might even resurface
with your survivor's tenacity, with that tone of your voice
saying *Listen to me*.

Then you'd gasp to final silence, a look of surprise,
and leave me just that still, red light –
like a swimmer's warning.

Kathryn Simmonds

Transvestite in the Library

You're weighted on one heel
at the enquiry desk, hipless
and hard-breasted,
wearing something short
and silver-glittered;
nothing printed on a page
could fascinate like you.

When I rise to leave I pass you
kneeling on your rower's legs
beside ROMANCE –
but can't make out
the title in your hands.

Where are you in the formula,
the hero-heroine cliché?

Or are you, with a pencil tip
far sharper than my stranger's stare,
swiftly writing yourself in?

Difficult Scene in a Hospital Room

You play my father, though I hardly
recognize you in your costume
of pyjamas and bewilderment.
The nurses know their lines but we
have not rehearsed for this and so
we improvise, read snippets from
the newspapers, retell old jokes.

A lighting change: the sun is cued
to set behind your head
freeze-framing you in bronze.

Later, in the cutting-room,
they'll put in an adagio,
but this will not be edited –
the moment when you look at me
and then away.

Before I turn to exit, leaving you
spot-lit beneath a creaking wall light,
you press my hand
but do not make a speech.

I want to double-check the script
beside your bed, I want to find out
how this ends, how many scenes
we have like this. But it has gone,
so has the makeup they have used
to age you with.

Models

One by one
they enter light,
pale-armed,
pod-chested,
weirdly dressed in fabrics
from the underworld.
They've come of age
too soon
and move along
their brilliant strip
of summertime,
no longer seeking out
their mothers' faces
in the crowd.
They are alone and wear
the beauty of the dead.
Just before the drop
they pause,
then turn away.
Their mouths are longed for,
bitter as a single
pomegranate seed.

Vincent De Souza

Doll's Cannibal Friend

A cycle of same dramas
Pour from the little girl,
Into a slim body of plastic;
Barbie's fed a cheap-talk script.

Blonde with a mane of curls,
She's still in her dumb silence;
The gargantuan puppy-fat girl
Has Barbie traits on tap.

Between fantasy games,
The girl barely gets older;
She'll bide her time, wise-up
Into a dress size of her own;

Her swoon is a play perfection,
She cooks Barbie in a tribal pan:
Doubled-up, catwalk legs in the air,
A doll to consume, making you want;

Seasoned with tiny accessories,
Tiara, handbag and princess shoes.
The girl's growing pains stir,
Too real to thicken dry stew;

Barbie is stoic till the end,
A show-off, stiff fascist in pink,
Her heady smile served up
When hot lips split.

Getting It from the Adequate Mirror

Soho bar people, sliding in a still life,
Walkers cross the screen in my head;
Full frontal, the illuminated street,
An evolving copy of the same view
Kept in motion on the wall mirror.

In ornate gold and virtuously clean,
At an angle of ten degrees to the eye;
Each pelvis is dressed, limp arms hang,
A shaft of light points down at shoes,
Smoke gets blown at a haze of gender.

Males kiss cheeks, exaggerate embraces;
A drinker with a leg in plaster is flirting,
Eyes widen, ovals of an expanding mouth.
Most of us stare at the jeep parked outside;
The one in full leathers, easy at the entrance.

Against Adam

I wasn't.
When he crashed his motorcycle,
His skull caved, the helmet shell
Capped on vanity and persisting youth;
Still in control, he slipped it off,
And blacked-out in hospital,
Brains spilling from the alarming hole;
How he loved to recount
The way they patched his head,
Inserting an imperfect length of his rib.

After whiskeys, he treated his Eve like shit;
Taking the turn of a reptile deviant,
He did stuff to her – demonic slithers,
The rough or angelic avoid in sex.
She lived all right, grew near his thinking,
Curled in the chamber of dented bone;
Furious lover, she left and returned to abuse;
She couldn't move a limb before she died;
I need nothing to do with hate,
I saw him visit her, kind as any Satan.

Place of Forgiveness Somewhere in a Child

The world breezed through her hair,
And she blew soap bubbles
In its sensible face;
For more than one summer,
A sun appeared at random,
Glancing on her floral dress.

She was never quite herself
In the run of new months;
A sleeve began to show her wrist,

Eager, rising high on her toes,
She mocked the quiet of bedtime,
Tame shadows in the landing light.

Could a moment in her past life
Hold the seed of what happened?
The reports made us picture her,
Caught in a whirl of panic and lashes,
An adult attacker with sour scent;
A few feet away, the arrival of luck.

Safety stripped to its garish innards,
This eternity of terror and no time
To summon the names of her dolls;
Her soft toys, a mocking chain of devils,
Indulgent cuddles rebelled against her,
Abandoned by absent mum and dad,
In part, she set the tone of this horror.

> *For two weeks, her remains lay*
> *In a shallow woodland grave;*
> *On hands and knees,*
> *They searched for tiny fibres,*
> *Clues mixed with the rhythm*
> *Of A-road traffic, moving north.*

Once, her small hands were good
At clutching pencils and crayons;
One day and then another,
She'd do her copies of this world:
Kind sun, often with a human face,
Trees like uncles, pillars beside her,
Bare landscapes, too young for threats;
A skirt was a slab of favoured colour,
Her self portraits, flooded in smiles.

Towards the Abattoir

The two-foot wooden fence
Is fair at being itself,
Just as the grass
Consumes the space
Needed by a mass of nettles;
Down the road
Is the abattoir gate.
The stench is thick enough
To cut like cake;
I am inclined to feel sick,
But this day,
The disgust has its place.
It belongs
With the boredom of girls,
Their laughs in line at the bus stop;
I can see a silver Audi
With a window one third down.
From where I sit,
The unit of steel, chrome and plastic,
Is tremendous as any living form;
A woman walks her Highland terrier
To and from the abattoir.
She moves with a lilting balance,
Her steps neat as those of her dog;
No other moments will work like this.

Julian Stannard

Lengths

We take to the water for ease
but some moronic brute is
chasing lengths like a salaryman.

The next time his feet spear
into my ribs I will have to holler.
But why not head for calmer waters,

the slow lane of curious bathing caps
where drowning is always a chance
where the thigh of the pool is peace?

Riviera

We hid under the tunnel in *Via Milano*
to escape from the thunder
and the whiplash of lightning and rain.
Just three chairs holding the water back.

And then the slow climb into the hills
the wipers playing their music of nerves,
the olives sluiced, cleansed, waiting
for that hot god that comes after storms . . .

The lightning weaker now, less frequent
distant lights leaning on the villages:
Calderina, Castello, Serreta, Gorleri
suddenly broadened and held by arrows of mauve

before the folding in of shuttered rooms
dark, tense, moody spaces
the bloated icon, *la noia*, bitterness
the fruit that's always lusty in the mouth . . .

Via San Luca

Bars against the window
and we were paying for it . . .

Our ramshackle flat over the ships
and everything we touched was broken.

Every month our landlord,
an ex-fascist with a terrifying bladder,
took us out to assuage his guilt.

Sunbathing was a painstaking trip
onto a narrow roof, gawped at
and pecked by libidinous pigeons.

For six months
I was stoned on cheap grass
listening to Wynton Marsalis
and George, the *sine qua non*
of the public school system,
losing his virginity repeatedly
from under and over the roofs.

Stucco

I was your drunken Saxon
in your pretty Italian labyrinth

and when I sat on your doorstep of marble
you slapped my face and kissed me

but not necessarily in that order
and we agreed to hang around together

among the gifts of dogs and the stucco
the debris of mercantile grandeur

and now all you give me are snatches
of sleep and a tribe of children

who have come screaming out of history
with such fluted lyrical voices.

Ballo

Enzo has ducked down with the grass cutter.
Izio, the electrician, has gone Hawaiian.
Marilena, rich in houses, has beautiful hair.

The lady from Milan doesn't like *negri*
but she likes the strange vacuum of August
and she believes in the power of prayer.

Susanna in Venice since '68 –
her son is dancing with the thin blond girlfriend.
Sie sprechen Deutsch in piazza.

The old men are smoking like Turks
and always shouting, *Pino* is hawking his *Olivetti*.
No space for hiatus in dialect.

The blackshirt is gangly with cropped hair,
he is wearing braces with the faces of the *Duce*,
he is teaching his son how to tango.

My sad wife is ladling out sangria
and taking money for the *ballo, ah the ballo . . .!*
Clemé is spilling figs from her pockets.

And there's *Bruno* the rabbit-catcher,
the barber, the olive-bottler,
the voyager, gerontion ball-breaker . . .

My wife is *daunsinge* with *Izio*
gliding round and round and round the *ballo*
I am watching his hand on her arse.

After the *ballo* we stack the chairs, tables
and take a car to the sea; we strip and swim.
And because it is dark we are laughing.

Priscilla Stanton

Pageantry

We'd only been lovers for sixteen hours
that Christmas the train dropped us at Ely.
And among the exhaust-coughing cars, among
the lights bleeding sap in the blue cold,

we stirred like two halves of a dance,
no routine so deep as memory still feeling,
the warm domestic peace of a body well used,
the open possibility, always, of touching you

that I felt across high shelves of a stall,
that I knew even in the eyes of the vendor –
(he placed three pounds change in my palm;
you stood in the moving people, in the snow) –

all things Outside are only the bare back
of our private, foetal curl. And when
in the fields, the darkness fallows, softly,
with feather strokes, merging the spruces,

in Ely Cathedral, the candles are kindled,
plump oranges are placed in the palms
of children and priests and anxious mums.
But there is one other, with us, in the shadows –

a woman leaning on the last pew. She turns to look
just as you slip your fingers beneath my blouse.
Her eyes – raw, red – follow your hand;
they are pacified, deep in the peace that descends

long after crying. They stare; you murmur,
'That was *my* part every year.' Miles above
the sagging strata of incense and coughs,
the vaulted beams conjoin in air cold as stone.

It's only a second. You are buying tickets home.
I wait for you by the door to the platform.
You turn and smile, as if to say, I won't be long.
And I stare back, with no more recognition or love

than I feel for a stranger or a steel girder.
It's only a second. Through the darkness,
the carriage rattles swiftly on. And I cling to you
like a new bride, like you might disappear.

The Quiet

I find I like
the quiet now,
the empty house,
the pause between
the lorries going by
out in the street.

I find I like
the hugging-tight
of your absence,
the hours when the phone
steeps in silence,
the crackle of heat
through pipes
the only sound.

Loosing you
no longer shadows
like a sickle
around my heart.
Months it has taken
to trickle
deeper
down –
it is a firm,
rooted thing,
a stomach-succoured tuber,
the size of your hand.

One afternoon
in May you rang.
I listened
to the metal trills
dissipate
like the cries of swallows
breaching into air.
Then it was
quiet again.

Crude Harvest

I listen to you in the unlit kitchen,
I see you in the shadows festered
by a thermostat turned far to red.
I know you just returning from
the snow, and a meeting that ran
far too late at church. And I know why
you don't remove your car right away,

why you lean (the dog whines, afraid)
for a long time against the counter,
silent in your green, knee-length parka.
You look like a beleaguered gumdrop,
you look like a beautiful woman,
who is still in love, past any chance
at fifty-two. You mention his hands.

And I see you stacking folding chairs
in the basement afterwards – After –
in the Lysol-reeking cold, in the litter
of construction paper and glitter,
where seeing a brown, slightly ovulated ark
and a pink hand of God
momentarily foils your smile

to the minister's air-stewardess wife
sweeping in the corner. It is absurd.
Tonight, you tell me, you were caught,
off-guard and unprepared.
At the meeting of council members
and concerned parishioners,
you were just about to suggest that –

but then he came in,
and your voice suddenly went flat.
'Because it hurts too much sometimes,

to try to pretend.' Without looking, you knew
the exact location of his body, two chairs
to the left, or passing by the water-cooler.
You knew it like a condensed choir –

Who is the third who always walks beside you? –
you knew it like a monument to the rare
moment when silence buckles
to the un-worded, indrawn breath,
'This is . . . This is . . .' And you knew it
like the thing you must never ever
allow yourself to need more than, well . . .

'God makes good come out of your pain,'
you say, turning on the light and taking
the frozen lasagne out of the plastic.
The oven door shuts with a bang.
'Take your coat off, why don't you? Jesus.'
I refuse to extract a moral,
a gold-plated kernel, some product

of wincing intellect and retrospect
from this – because *this* is too subtle,
this is too difficult, too full of love,
too full of age and the pillow taste
of dry, early bedtime crying –
too full of you, and you are my mother.
If you won't scream, then I will.

Kernels don't come from something
as soft and as flowing
as white clothes, left lying
where they fell on the stone floor.
They were afraid to speak.
Trembling and bewildered,
*the women ran away.**
* *Mark 16:8*

Passed-over

Pushing the wire-carriage
through automatic doors,
the bales of winter light did not
freeze after flooding
the whites of your eyes;
we followed after, giggling
and carrying plastic bags.

On the porch before dark,
playing Monopoly
(sounds of a suburban swamp
strike only partial fear),
you did not *really* forget to roll;
a new husband sat inside,
watching television alone.

And on Saturday nights,
your teenagers both gone,
the yellow kitchen was not,
for more than a moment at least,
the cell of an acquiesced heart;
you heard the wind blowing
over the honed land, and hurt.

But yesterday I came upon you
paused on the sunny stair
by the sudden shift
of old fear, loose as flour,
from the place it has been kept;
pine planks creaked beneath
the postponement of your next step.

Mom? But then you hurried
rather soundlessly down the rest.

Andrew Waterhouse

In the Living Room
i.m. Alan Richardson

My friend, I imagine you, slowly moving
between objects, touching a photograph
of your father, your daughter's painting
of a sunrise, the cones in a summer hearth.

I see you stoop over yellow flowers,
freshly cut, half-smile with their scent;
I see you pick an apple from the bowl, bite;
I see you turn up the volume and a hero sings:

you breathe in, breathe out, you breathe in,
breathe out; as the moon rises
over rooftops, settles in the blackness
of your window, to be observed, unflinching:

the birth marks, craters, too familiar details.
My friend, I see your white face; your good, white face.

Photograph

udcloudcloudcloudcloudcloudcloudcloudcloudcloudcloudclou
dcloudskyskyskyskycloudcloudcloudcloudcloudcloudcloudjetcl
oudcloudcloudskydaymoonskycloudcloudcloudcloudcloudclou
cloudcloudcloudcloudcloudcloudcloudcloudcloudpossiblesunc
oudhelicopterclourainrainrainraincloudcloudcloudcloudcloudcl
udcloudcloudcloudrainrainrainraindcloudcloudhillcloudcloudcl
dhillcloudcloudcloudrainrainrainrcloudcloudhillhillhillcloudclo
illhilldwoodwoodwoodwoodwoodwoodhillhillhillhillhillhillhill
lhillhillhillhillwoodwoodwoodwoodwoodhillhillhillhillhillhillhil
lhwoodwoodfieldfieldvillagevillagerivervillagevillagefieldtankfi
dwoodwoodfieldfieldfieldvillagevillagerivervillagefieldfieldfield
dwoodwoodvillagevillagevillagerivervillagefieldsmellbadsmells
odwoodvillagevillagesmokevillagerivervillagefieldholeholefield
dwoodwoodvillagevillagevillagevillagerivervillagevilfibadsmell
woodwooillagesmokevillagevillagesmokebodyvillagefieldfhole
menmenmenwoodwovillagevillagevillagevillagerivervillagevfiel
menbodiesmenwoodwoovillagesmokevillagevillagerivervillagev
menbodiesmendwoodwoodlagevillagevillagesmokvillagerivevil
menmenmenoodwoodwoodillagevillagevillagevillagevillagriver
oodwoodwoodwoodwoodwillagevillagevillagevillagerivervillag

Bath Time
for Hala

The ceiling is blue and the walls are yellow;
hanging, is a shoal of red and green fish,
turning so slowly, turning so slowly;
among your soaps and creams rest oyster shells,
also limpets and a line of seahorses
ride up towards the true mirror as we float
together in your large bath, steam rising
around us and I sink between your legs,
lean back against your breasts and smiling
you pour water over my face, my hair,
again and again as if I had just emerged,
needing to be woken up and well cleansed
before you could help me onto dry land.

Poem in Heavy Rain

Our tent breathing the wind
and the downpour pouring down;
each drop heard, only dots,
encoded, nonsense
from a much higher place

and I feel the pressure rising
all around us and I listen to the stream
cutting deeper and closer
and you sleep-cry a message:
something important about love, about love.

The Beach at Newton

A small stream talks to the ocean,
having cut left and right through the dunes,
now broadening, losing depth, collecting the sun

and I stop where the flow meets the waves,
in dispute over well-ribbed sand,
as a gull settles, folds, unfolds;

then drifts off on the wind,
loaded with quiet, heading further north
where it is darker sooner; and this was not intended

to be here without you at the stream's mouth,
in December, listening to the lowering surf.

Emily Wills

Interrogation

Where, precisely, did you find it?
What was it doing at the time? Did it ask
to be taken? Can you describe
identifying features? (Black/white,
plastic, punctured.)

Did you alter it in any
significant way? (Patch over holes,
compress valve, inflate
until breathless.) Who took it
to the sea? Did you obtain informed
consent? How was the tide? The wind?
(Quicksilver, ironing fast the sand.)

Who else was there? (Throwing,
calling, catching.) Were there witnesses?
(Two swimmers, just out of depth, watching
the child running, reaching, heartbeating black
on silver, the others tense and stilled.)

Was it reflected sun, or blown ball, upsail
full speed past swimmers, beyond waves?
How did it leave you? (Blackpaper silhouette,
turned back, emptied.)

Who waits, with open arms
on the other side of the sea?

Developing the Negative

I did not see low sun
lighting you pale between
two uncut fields. The sky
was neither blue not high nor red.

I did not know you pale, becoming
breath, becoming light;
forgot to write down every word
or draw your smile.

I was not that red-blue light
drawing you uphill, breathless, into
slow falling sun. Yet now I hold
this uncut sky between
my breathing hands

and see, as if written down
in this high field, our pale
forgetting words, and how
we tried to smile.

Statistics

like the radio, can make you believe
anything. They say there are more
cut wrists, more paracetamol regretted,
not, as you might expect,
in grey-man's-land November, overdrawn
burst-pipe January,
but in the spring.

Something about hours of light,
hibernation, disputed theories
of evolution, melatonin, evidence,

proof. But what they haven't seen
is this: the terrible labouring of so much
green through last year's slough of leaves,
the newborn, newblown sky
gull-screaming for response.
Or these insistent mornings, glittering
newgreen, tight pink, yellow crocus point.

Most of all, it's that low sun, how last year's
fingerprints reproach on every glass,
and dust furs thick enough to write in.
The radio patters on. Probability, significance
or none; a few degrees of freedom,
how we're a standard curve, not daring
far from reassuring axes x and y and *home*
meaning this may be chance,
or belief, or words
fingered in white dust.

Judging Distances

I see you from years after,
crouched with your child
on bony soil; your hut resisting
brown river's pull on slanting land.
You have something to sell
in a small basket, but your face
is emptied of all but waiting.
Passing coffee, coins, our hands
collided without touch, as if we met
distorted by underwater light
bent at bright interface of different air.

I know this common load
of a child, loosened with sleep,
I have sweated with birth,
let down still-dark mornings' milk
to drown his endless cry.

I've learned your words for *child*,
for *hunger*, *body*, *blood*;
rehearsed warm singing sounds
for *reaching*, *meeting*, *knowing* –
All speech erodes like soil, leaving
silent desert space between us.

Woman, child, basket, home,
are always there, clearly defined
but still too small among difficult hills
measured with one eye closed and pencil
huge against unshaded midday white.

The Recipe for Marmalade

is coded in my genes, a gift
I can't refuse. As birds fly south
with shrinking light, so pale grey
January afternoons induce this need
for bitter unwaxed oranges,
glinting sugar landslides,
windows dribbling steam.
The script copperplates warnings,
for sweetness boils hotter,
blood drips thicker than water.
Don't ask; it's the recipe
the family use. Don't touch;
old blades can skin you raw.

Tough sunless fruit
collapses with heat, flabby peel
old woman's skin under the knife.
Grandmother's wooden spoon
worn smooth and black, stirs
quilted liquid, whispered histories.

And yet she has handed down
these things: faith, that bitterness
transform to a year of sweet; hope
for a good firm set, and always
her steady stirring grip, fearless
through molten amber.

Helen Wilson

Playing Titanic

Here is my boy in the bath,
playing his favourite game.
In this warm womb world
a bubble mountain looms,
and the plastic ship tips,
until all the little people slip
into the swallowing sea.
Strange, how my son delights in death,
not a baby now, but nemesis,
small laughing god of chaos.

Here is his mother,
one hand trailing the water,
bored and fickle as Hera
troubling the pool of the mortals.
Tired of paradise I
too would tip and rip
apart my world for a kiss,
and would risk all this
for your face, your voice,
for the dangerous illusion of choice.

The New World

My young son sits in his Indian tent
looking out at the world with calm satisfaction.
For him huge herds of buffalo still roam,
acres of maize thrive, while the big sky
is bountiful and permanent.
With Wakan Tanka at his side he can smile
at the sweetness of the rains,
the certainty of the returning sun.
His dreams do not show him the ships
driving relentlessly on towards the shore,
loaded with hopes and a terrible hunger.
Bringing some beads. Great bagfuls of words.

Abbaye de Bonne Esperance

My father brought me here
when the world was dark.
He had nothing to say and so,
with a hand on my shoulder,
he pointed into the stillness.
I have always had trouble with stars,
but struggled to see the dragons
and dancers, dogs and gods he saw.
I gave him this like a kiss
before I turned and went in.
Here it is much the same as at home.
While the women work, or gather quiet at night,
the priest stands, like any man by the fire,
to tell the old tale, and we hear again
how the son is loved most.
As I lie awake at night I imagine
those other myths emerging over my head,
and by day live in hope on this hill.

Morgan Yasbincek

endodontics

the plan is, he says, to excavate
the antagonist i've harboured for years

it has secured higher ground
and dug in

this is a surgical manoeuvre
the guerrilla, disarmed by antibiotics,
will be excised in a single operation

my tooth disappears in the flood
the red, bloody hole is screened
in his glasses

drowned bone is located by the scalpel
and his yellow latex gloves are stained to the
first joint of each digit

this tight metaphor won't stretch enough
to include my eyes, my body, my fear

only my blood, which springs into the frames
above his mask from some numb place

light on her belly

a full white globe shudders
as she dries herself, her hair all quills
her weighty breasts drag skin away
from her clavicle, she sniffs

props one leg forward under
the huge dome and the blow-out
of her breasts, in the shape of this
her bones, my sister

hot tap bites her hip, we watch the
space of a window, a memory of a man
who entered our house on bags of trinkets
and begged her kisses

in her bedroom
a harmonised fuzz of murmurs twists behind the door
nested like spiny caterpillars

in that talk aliens would come in jesus' spaceship

burn our eyes
out of their sockets, melt our socks on the line

at eleven she wanted to go with him, to be one
of the chosen and she waited, kept her secret, the
only one she never told, because telling would
mean being left behind

as she towels the body she shares
with another beginning

her heavy body swings into
the gravity of our talk

a doorknob in her home
teatowel over the dishes
the horrifying stars

the tie of her mouth is the same
walking to school with me day after day
grey bags held in our armpit, swaggering
over the footpath, unable to tell me that tonight
they might come for my eyes

if

you touched me my ribs
would shatter and my heart
would fall through its storm
and flare like a coal
caught in a gas jet

i know the course set by your eyes
and, as fire is contagious, i need

an ocean, something southern and polar
to put me out, pat salt over my rawness
cauterize my weakness, spume a tender
skin of foamy calm, snuff out the panic

touch every part, every part

fuck you eros

and your eternal flame
i'm a burnt fuel

dead coal alive with your heat
flare when you come near
in dayglo orange

and you can fly because i never knew
what the exchange could make of me

because my heart is a plum
divided by a curve, purple
in its holding, lippy, tight and
ready for wounding
and my blood
is as intent
as a line of risen meerkats

eleven

the owl arrives in the afternoon
i am stuffing a great cloud of washing into the machine
she is picking oranges at the side of the house,
releasing them into cream and blue cracked buckets
she calls
i'm busy with detergent and a loose dial
she is running and shouting
a white, beaked heart has alighted on the pergola
addressed her
even though it is day
even though she's only eleven

Miranda Yates

There Are Many Ways to Leave a Millionaire and This Is One

Be French and 36 and not pregnant again.
Peel off the thigh-high boots that cost him an arm and a leg,
Wrestle your mock-croc coat into the ornamental pond,
Watch it sink under thick algae skin.

The snow is light as a falling eyelash.
The hothouse is a long summer bottled in glass
Three miles – longer than you ever thought you'd have to walk again.

Your husband is on a seed-collecting mission in Uganda.
Imagine a thousand deaths in shades of jungly green –
Stung, stunned, man-trapped, cooked as sacrificial meat,
His chest is a bloody trampoline for the gorillas,
All that's left is a heap of bones licked clean.

It won't work, but run a stilleto heel against your wrist,
Knock, knock your boot against the glass
To catch the attention of the rare coal orchid,
Fumbled and abused into life and born to be named after you.

Inside there's a chair of mossy wicker and a radio left on.
You hear polite applause brush the yellow teeth of a piano.
You are colder than winter. Take your shoe to each pane of glass.
Watch the rains come to shatter the Amazon.

In the Back Garden with the Lead Pencil

My mother has a soft blue spot like a permanent bruise on her
                                                                left buttock
From where she was pricked with an HB pencil
Kept in the breast pocket of my father's sports jacket.

He was running with her in his arms, round and round the garden
Like a big finger tracing circles on a dainty palm.
The bundle of her flesh was soft as a basket of laundry

My grandmother rests two mugs of brick-red tea on the coal
                                                                bunker,
leaving the *young people* to their own devices.
The pond is there, before the rippling muscle of fish were
                                                                caught and entrusted

To a cousin from Congleton and the water drained, for the
                                                                safety of grandchildren.
The flower borders stink, as they always would, of horse muck
Collected from the lane of trampled grass backing into
                                                                Maggorty Wood.

Flies flinch on the sick warmth of the compost heap
When my mother squeals as she's pierced and marked
Indelibly and their love becomes lead;

Not uncommon but stout, heavy and resistant to corrosion.
The lead that sketched and shaded in me and my brother,
the sturdy plumbing that's buried inside us.

Dense, prehistoric and impossible to live up to,
The reason we both left home so late and so reluctantly.

Savonarolla
Savonarolla was the ascetic priest responsible for the Fire of the Vanities

Savonarolla was my neighbour's boy,
Not so much hit but beaten bloody and half-senseless by the
                                                    ugly stick.
His cheeks were as hollow as any pit of Inferno,
With great nostrils for sniffing out sin – there was something
                                                    about him.
When I felt the dead weight of his gaze, my painted lips hung
                                                    heavy on my
face and my charm bracelet felt laden as a curse
Three times a day he filled an iron bath from the groaning
                                                    cistern
Pink maggot scrubbing himself out with pig's bristle
His soul seemed already nailed to his coffin.

He had a knack for finding things:
Missing watches, lucky handkerchiefs, lost brooches
Bad wives would send him up the long leg of Italy
To seek out their wedding rings.
If you asked him for the secret, how he did it, he said
He could feel the heat rising from our precious things.

*

He grew up, if those are the right words for a man who is
                                                    ancient from birth.
He took the cloth, took orders, took a diet of breadcrumbs
                                                    and spikes under the surplus.
I used to see him slipping out into the soft cowl of the
                                                    Florentine darkness.
We would watch him preach, big family day out with sandwiches.
He'd choose the Duomos with the best acoustics and give us hell
His tongue licking our hearts like cold flame, tasting our sin
Afterwards my hands felt as light and fluttery as doves' wings
And my rings would have slipped from my fingers into my pockets.

*

The flames started with a stinky pyre of necklaces on a
                                                flammable hassock
Then came the dust of ancestors in jewelled caskets,
Pearls blackening into rosary beads and whole fireplaces finding
                                                their match,
Pianos sounded off against an axe, mirrored doors opened into
                                                hell's jaws.

The sky was charcoal grey for weeks and my neighbour
Found the face of Christ, drawn in soot across her sheets.

Marble Dust

Father started building my tomb on the day I was born.
He hires workers whose dusty boots march
Like woken statues through my prayers and out of the Amen.
The lifeline on my right palm is thin as a grass snick
And when they burned my birthcharts, the parchment stank like
The breath of rotten corpses and fire bled until they called in an
                                                exorcist.
On each of my saints' days a cargo of pink sunset marble
Arrives cold and chattering on the back of a cart.
On my sixteenth they put up the scaffolding.
Workers buzzed like flies on its skeleton.
No expense will be spared –
Frescoes, tableaux and statues of fat-buttocked angels,
Jewelled arches raised like the eyebrows of Croesus
While stairs run riot like princesses in an empty palace
And stone gods with squirting phalluses stand in relief.

This morning Florence's air is tender as a box
Of coloured pastels, rubbed into itself with one finger.
The workers doff their caps and watch the mist kissing my ankles.
Four storeys up the artist, commissioned to build my coffin,
Makes light of gravity – a bad-tempered spec, he paces as if
He painted the contours of the sky and is unhappy
When he spits, for an airborne second I see the webbed wing
                                        of an angel
They say his wet nurse carried marble dust in her breasts.
He holds his hands up to get things in perspective.

Barefoot inside my tomb when it's all but finished,
The makeshift ceiling billows like a lung
Any day we're expecting red mosaic pieces from Arezzo
On the walls, a cruel twist of brambles waits for roses.
His statues are all limbs and gown
But with faces clear and naked as the moon
In the centre is a perfect block of egg-white marble
Tomorrow the artist comes to cut me free.

Notes on Contributors

Patricia Adelman was born and raised in the Yorkshire minefields and is now a grandmother living in Bath. After nursing, marriage, teaching and degree studies, she at last came to what had been waiting for her serious attention. For this late-achieving 'Eng Lit' graduate poetry composition has involved much unravelling and knitting up – not such an easy task. Patricia now has poems published in magazines, anthologies, and a first collection out later this year with Flarestack Publishing.

Christoher Allan was born in Cheshire and spent his youth as an athlete and a follower of Tranmere Rovers. He became interested in poetry in the late 1970s and began writing in the late 1980s. He was encouraged by Matthew Sweeney and Roger Garfitt when they were poets-in-residence in Worcestersire in the early 1990s. His poems have recently been published in *Rialto, Fire, Other Poetry* and *Smiths Knoll*. A collection, *Dancing in Paper Trousers*, was published in 1996.

Liz Almond lives in Hebden Bridge, West Yorkshire and teaches creative writing at Manchester Metropolitan University. Her work has been published in magazines including *Ambit, Cyphers* and *Writing Women* and also in two anthologies: *The Long Pale Corridor*, published by Bloodaxe, and *Generations* published by Penguin. A pamphlet, *Art Is Only A Boy's Name*, was published by Crocus Books in 1995.

Paul Batchelor can hear nothing but answering machines, babies crying, bare feet stomping on the floor, and Sleepy John Estes. Across the street the dogs are barking. It is dark and always dark.

Roy Blackman, a 1993 Hawthornden Fellow, lives in Suffolk. He co-edits the poetry magazine *Smiths Knoll*, is secretary for the Aldeburgh Poetry Trust and an Open College of the Arts tutor. After a Ph.D. in marine zoology he realized that choosing science at thirteen was a mistake. A happy ten years produced an Open University First Class Honours BA which started him writing again after twenty years. Rockingham published his first collection *As Lords Expected* (not about cricket) in 1996 and he's now seeking a publisher for a second.

Lawrence Bradby lives in Norwich and teaches geography with the Open University. He is currently working on a collaborative project producing poems which address the city's vanished doorways.

Deborah Chivers is a creative writing tutor and Ph.D. student at Cardiff University. She is currently completing her first collection of poetry, bringing together many poems that have appeared individually in literary magazines and competition anthologies. She also writes short stories using the name Deborah Davies. Stories from her new collection have won a national prize, been broadcast on BBC Radio 4 and published in *Mslexia*.

Clare Crossman was born in Kent in 1954. Her first collection of poetry, *Landscapes*, was published by Redbeck Press in 1996. She started writing seriously when she was thirty: community theatre plays at the Dukes Playhouse in Lancaster and a sequence of poems that was published as part of the city's Literature Festival. She has been included in several anthologies, including *The Long Pale Corridor* (Bloodaxe, 1996), and a poetry film *In the Mind of Man* (Nick May, 2000, Northern Arts). In 1999 Clare was awarded a Hawthornden Fellowship. She runs writing workshops for older people, children and those with mental health problems.

David Evans is a graduate of Norwich School of Art & Design, and is working for a Ph.D. in performance writing at Dartington College of Arts. His poetry has been published in *Smiths Knoll*, *Birdsuit* and *Reactions*.

Ivy Garlitz was born in Florida and lived in Poland and Germany before settling in Britain. She has been a featured poet in *Thumbscrew*, and her poems have appeared in *Poetry Review*, *The Rialto*, *The Honest Ulsterman* and other magazines. She was shortlisted for the 2000 Geoffrey Dearmer Prize. Her webcam project was one of the winners of the Showcase competition for innovative websites featured on BBC2's *The Net*. Ivy's first pamphlet, *A Better Life*, is published by the Bay Press.

Hannah Godfrey was born in Billericay in 1977. She studied literature and philosophy at the University of East Anglia and begins an MA in modern and contemporary poetry at Bristol University in autumn 2001. Since graduating she has worked as a bookseller, finance officer, masseuse, and charity fundraiser; she has also been on an expedition to Namibia and picked strawberries in Denmark.

Mark Haddon has written fourteen books for children and won two BAFTAs for his TV scriptwriting. He has just completed a novel, *Light*, and is working on a play about Helen of Troy for BBC Radio 4 and a comedy drama, *Hot Cakes*, for BBC television. His poetry has been published in various magazines and he was twice shortlisted for 2000's Arvon Prize.

Danny Hardisty is currently researching a Ph.D. on Philip Larkin at the University of East Anglia. These are his first published poems

Ramona Herdman has just completed an MA in poetry at UEA. She has had poems published in *Staple*, *The Rialto*, *The Reator*, *Reactions* and *Thumbscrew*, as well as in the UEA *<text>* series. Her poetry was discussed in the Masterclass at the Aldeburgh Poetry Festival 2000. She lives in Norwich.

Yannick Hill was born in Basel, Switzerland, in 1980. His mother tongue is Swiss-German; his father tongue is English. He lives in Devon. He learnt to walk when he was one. He learnt to like family walks when he was thirteen. He would like a dog. He would like a dog to take him for walks.

Andrea C Holland teaches creative writing at UEA and at Norwich School of Art & Design. She is also currently editor of the literary anthology, *Birdsuit*, and when not parenting, teaching or editing, she is a writer of poems. Publications include *New Writing 10*, *The Rialto*, *Other Poetry*, *The Greensboro Review* and other American publications. Her collection, *Borrowed*, is looking for a publisher. She lives in Norwich with her son.

Matthew Hollis was born in Norwich in 1971 and works as an editor for the Oxford University Press. He won an Eric Gregory Award in 1999, and is co-editor (with W. N. Herbert) of *Strong Words: Modern Poets on Modern Poetry* (Bloodaxe, 2000).

Helen Ivory was born in Luton in 1969 and currently lives in rural Norfolk. She has worked in shops, behind bars and with several thousand free-range hens. She has studied painting and photography and has a degree in cultural studies from Norwich School of Art. In 1999 she won an Eric Gregory Award. She has published in *Ambit*, *New Writing 10*, *Reactions* and *Orbis*. Her first collection, *The Double Life of Clocks*, will be published by Bloodaxe in 2002.

Jessica Jacobs is currently completing her final year at Smith College, USA. She has written for several American newspapers and magazines. After graduation she hopes to waitress in Greece or do something else equally worthwhile. These are her first published poems.

Christopher James is 26, enjoys running, beer and playing the banjo. Since completing an MA in creative writing at UEA he has lived in Darlington, Leeds and London, where he now works as a children's book editor. His influences include Bruce Chatwin, Keith Douglas and Bruce Springsteen.

James Knox Whittet was born and brought up on the Hebridean island of Islay. After leaving school, he worked as a gardener at Dunrobin Castle in the Highlands. He then enrolled at Scotland's adult residential college, Newbatle Abbey, the first principal of which was the Orcadian poet Edwin Muir, and went on to read english at Cambridge. He began writing poetry seriously some four years ago after attending an Arvon course tutored by the Hebridean poet, Iain Crichton Smith.

Judith Lal was born in the Cotswolds in 1975. She has recently been shortlisted for an Eric Gregory Award and was winner of the New Writer 2000 Poetry Prize. Her first collection, *The Origami Garden*, is due to appear in an anthology of New British Poets published by Plantagenet Press in spring 2002. She lives in Norwich, and has just completed an MA in creative writing at UEA.

Katie Landon grew up in the Virginia suburbs of Washington, DC, and is now a senior, studying creative writing and english literature at the University of New Mexico in Albuquerque.

Sarah Law has a Ph.D. in mysticism and modernist women writers. She runs the Julian Centre in Norwich, and teaches creative writing with WEA and the Centre for Continuing Education at UEA. Her first collection, *Bliss Tangle*, was published by Stride in 1999. She has recently had work published in *Fire*, *The Paper*, and a poetry sequence, *The Baptism of the Neophytes*, can be viewed online at <www.unf.edu/mudlark/>. Work in an art, CD and writing project, *Constellations*, is forthcoming from Stride.

Nigel Lawrence was born in Leeds and is currently a student on the creative writing MA at UEA. He first started writing poetry as a teenager. Some work was published while at university, but he stopped writing soon after. His career then took him through a variety of jobs including chauffeur, teacher, journalist and senior posts in public relations. He began writing poetry again following two Arvon courses in the mid-1990s and won a commendation in the 1997 National Poetry Competition.

John McCullough lives in Brighton where he is currently researching a D.Phil thesis on early modern friendship in relation to Marlowe, Spenser and Drayton's poetry. He begins teaching English at the University of Sussex in 2001. His work has appeared in numerous magazines and anthologies including *Touch*, *Writing on Drugs* and *Sesame*.

Christine McNeill was born in Vienna and came to England in 1970. In 1993 Bloodaxe Books published her first collection, *Kissing the Night*. Many poems in that volume focused on her experience of growing up in postwar Vienna. Her recent work reflects her interest in the relationship between psychology, spirituality, and language. Currently she's engaged on a translation of Rilke's poems contained in *Das Stundenbuch*.

Julius Man has been writing for a few years now. In his poems he hopes to find a happy balance between the sound and the meaning. He's always lived and worked in Cheltenhamshire, so his writing tends to be very involved with the local area.

Jill Maughan was born in 1958 in Newcastle-upon-Tyne. She went to Sunderland University where she achieved a BA (Hons) in communication studies. Bloodaxe published her first collection of poems, *Ghosts at Four o'Clock*, and she won an Eric Gregory Award in 1987. Her poems have appeared in anthologies, including *New Women Poets* (ed. Carol Rumens, Bloodaxe, 1990), *The Gregory Anthology* (Hutchinson), and *Fourpack #1: Four from Northern Women* (Bloodaxe, 1986). HarperCollins published her first children's book, *The Deceivers*. After stints in journalism and social work, she is now a freelance writer

Andrew Mayne works as a schoolteacher and heads the english department at Manchester Grammar School. He has published several textbooks (*Considering Prose, Considering Drama, The Language Book*), some critical writing (a study of Conrad's *The Secret Agent*) and also student editions of plays (*The Winslow Boy, Loot*). He started sending poems to magazines at the end of 1998; his work has appeared recently in *Staple, Smiths Knoll, The Anglo-Welsh Review*.

Jenny Morris writes poetry and fiction. Her work has been published in magazines and anthologies in the UK, USA and Australia. She grew up in Yorkshire and Angus, and has since lived and taught in Norfolk, Dorset, Sussex, Kent, Surrey, Wiltshire, Hertfordshire, London, Germany and the Far East. She has a son and daughter, and now lives in Norwich.

James Oliver was born in a small village outside Norwich in 1959. In 1963 his family moved to the North Norfolk coast. He attended Paston Grammar School in North Walsham, followed by City College, Norwich and Bristol University. He started writing in 1983 while in mental hospital. Later, having fallen in love, a Buddhist friend suggested that he write poetry, which James has been doing steadily ever since.

Helen Oswald's poems have appeared in *Poetry Review, London Magazine, The Rialto* and *Poetry London*. In 1999, she was a winner of the Blue Nose Poet of the Year Competition and commended in the National Poetry Competition. Helen lives in Brighton and works for the trade union, Unison.

Dean Parkin was born in Suffolk and currently works for *The Rialto* poetry magazine and the Aldeburgh Poetry Trust. His poems have appeared in *Boomerang, Other Poetry, Seam, Smith's Knoll* and *Smoke*.

Simon Pettifar used to be a publisher but found himself turning into a writer. His collections, *Seawrack, Further Poems* and *Bhakti*, are, in Allen Ginsberg's happy phrase, 'all published in heaven', though individual poems have appeared in *Sunk Island Review, Gargoyle, still*, the *Daily Express, Gargoyle* (USA), *Babel* (Germany) and on the walls of his friends' bedrooms . Simon is also working on two prose collections: *Islands of the Present* (non-fiction) and *Tenderness*. He lives in Belgium.

Lynne Rees was born and brought up in South Wales but now lives in Kent and tutors creative writing for the University of Kent at Canterbury. She is an MA graduate of the University of Glamorgan and her poems have appeared in many literary journals including *New Welsh Review, Poetry Wales, The Rialto* and *Stand*. A selection of her work, including the title poem, was published in *Teaching a Chicken to Swim – New Writing from Glamorgan* (Seren, 2000).

Jacqui Rowe began writing poetry seriously in 1995, as part of an MA course in english linguistics. In 1998, David Hart, then Poet Laureate for Birmingham, chose one of her poems to open the Year of Arts organized by Birmingham Education Authority. Jacqui has since had work published by *Flarestack* and in *Mslexia*. She was shortlisted for the Ledbury Poetry Prize in 2000. She is Head of English and Fellow of the University of the First Age at a boys' technology college in Birmingham, and has a husband, a teenage daughter and a Gordon setter.

Sibyl Ruth's first poetry collection, *Nothing Personal*, was published in 1995 by Iron Press. Since then she's spent a year as Poet Laureate of Birmingham and has recently started writing drama. Her one-act play, *Mysterious Ways*, has been performed in London and Birmingham. Sibyl works at the Midlands Arts Centre organizing its literature programme, and continues to write poems.

Robert Seatter has twice been a prize-winner in the National Poetry Competition, and his work has also collected prizes in London Poetry, Peterloo, Housman, Manchester and Tabla poetry competitions, among others. His poems have appeared in publications including: *Poetry Wales*, *Ambit*, *Poetry London*, *Envoi*, *Staple*, *Stand*, *Smith's Knoll*, *Tabla*, *Blade*, and on the London buses. His work is featured in *Anvil New Poets 3* (May 2001) and in *Chalk Face Muse*. He studied English at Oxford University, and then worked as an EFL teacher, actor, and in publishing. He now lives in London and works at the BBC.

Kathryn Simmonds was born in Hertfordshire in 1972. She used to work in publishing, which influenced her decision to go backpacking around Australia. This year she will be studying on the creative writing MA at UEA.

Vincent De Souza studied english and philosophy at UEA. To pay the bills, he works as an advertising copywriter in London. Language and literature remain a passion and his work has appeared in anthologies, magazines and competitions. He has run workshops and is working with a co-writer on poetry episodes based on *Batman*, and a second on *Barbie*. He enjoys the challenge of building poems with a spontaneous, pictorial feel, his main watchword being directness.

Julian Stannard was born in 1962 and educated at the Universities of Exeter and Oxford. From 1987-1993 he taught at the University of Genoa and now lectures at Suffolk College, a college of UEA. His writing – poetry and criticism – has been published in magazines and journals such as *London Magazine*, *Ambit*, *Stand*, *Poetry Ireland Review*, *Oxford Poetry*, *Rialto*, *The Honest Ulsterman*, *Thumbscrew*, *Nuova Corrente* and the *PN Review*. His work appeared in Faber's introductory anthology *First Pressings*, and he has written a study of Fleur Adcock. *Rina's War*, a first collection, is published by Peterloo Poets.

Priscilla Stanton was born in Massachusetts in 1978. She attended Middlebury College, Vermont, but transferred to UEA to complete her degree in english and american literature. She is now studying at UEA for her MA in modernism. Priscilla is committed to furthering her knowledge of British TV and has recently discovered that Richard and Judy are actually married.

Andrew Waterhouse was born in Lincolnshire in 1958. He was a farm worker before studying environmental studies at university. He has lived in rural Northumberland for the last fifteen years and is now trying to write full-time. His first collection, *In*, appeared in May 2000 and went on to win the Forward Prize for Best First Collection. Andrew completed an MA in creative writing at Northumbria University in 1998. He is currently Writer in Residence at Woodhorn Colliery Museum near Ashington in Northumberland, and is working on a second collection.

Emily Wills is a full-time parent and part-time GP. She came to Gloucestershire via Cornwall and Malawi. Her first collection *Diverting the Sea* was published in 2000 by *The Rialto*.

Helen Wilson was born in 1959. She is an english lecturer in further education, and mother to five-year-old Tom. A writer all her life, she began to write more seriously after attending a course at the Hen House, Lincolnshire, in 1995, and has had poems published in *Lancashire Life* and *First Time*.

Morgan Yasbincek is a Western Australian writer. Her first collection of poetry, *night reversing*, won the 1997 Anne Elder Poetry Award and the 1997 Mary Gilmore Poetry Award. Her first novel, *liv*, was published by Fremantle Arts Centre Press in June 2000. In 1998 she travelled to the United Kingdom where she completed a residency at UEA. She teaches creative writing at Murdoch University and is currently taking a break from researching her Ph.D. to care for her baby daughter and develop her second collection of poetry.

Miranda Yates graduated from UEA in 1997 with an MA in creative writing. She divides her time between working as a press officer and arts reviewer for a local newspaper, writing and watering her plants.

The Litmus Test: Call for Submissions
Reactions 2002

Is your poetry acid or alkaline? As long as it isn't neutral, I'd like to hear from you . . .

The third edition of *Reactions* will appear in 2002. *Reactions* is a forum for new poetry by new poets. Submissions are therefore invited from writers who have had a first collection or pamphlet published (but not a second), and from those who have not yet reached that stage.

If you are interested in submitting work, please send five poems with an SAE to Esther Morgan at the School of English and American Studies, University of East Anglia, Norwich NR4 7TJ.

The poems you send:

- can be on any subject, in any style and of any length.

- should be written in English, but can be in translation.

- should be typed, with your name and address appearing clearly on each.

- must be your own original work.

- must not already be accepted for publication by any magazine (although poems which are due to appear in a first collection or anthology will be considered).

- should be accompanied by a covering letter which lists the titles of your poems, plus a short biography (of no more than 70 words).

- need to reach me no later than 31 March 2002.

- must be good.

PRETEXT

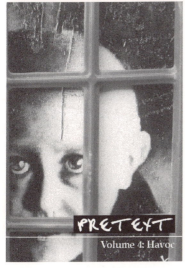

Volume 4: Havoc

Subscribe to UEA's new International Literary Magazine **Pretext** and save 25% on the cover price. Published twice a year, **Pretext** aims to become one of the most exciting and innovative new literary magazines on the market.

Volume 4 will be published in October 2001, containing: exclusive extracts from Lars von Trier's diary of filming *The Idiots*, an interview with W.G. Sebald; Sarah May on Macedonia; new poetry from John Burnside and George Szirtes; new fiction from Clare MacDonald, Ronan Bennett, Günther Kaip, Juan Goytisolo, and introducing Draco Maturana, among many others. Subscription copies cost only £6 including p&p, instead of the RRP of £7.99 Send or email your name and address to:

**Simon Brett,
Pretext Subscriptions,
English and American Studies,
University of East Anglia,
Norwich, NR4 7TJ
simon@penandinc.co.uk**

Your copy will be mailed to you in October 2001, along with a direct debit form. Subscribers will also be included on our mailing list and be updated regularly on our publications.

Pretext will be available in all good bookshops from November 2001.